No Ordinary Men

Dietrich Bonhoeffer and Hans von Dohnanyi, Resisters Against Hitler in Church and State

No Ordinary Men

Dietrich Bonhoeffer and Hans von Dohnanyi, Resisters Against Hitler in Church and State

Elisabeth Sifton and Fritz Stern

NEW YORK REVIEW BOOKS

New York

THIS IS A NEW YORK REVIEW BOOK

NO ORDINARY MEN
Copyright © 2013 by Elisabeth Sifton and Fritz Stern
Copyright © 2013 by NYREV, Inc.

Published by The New York Review of Books, 435 Hudson Street, Suite 300, New York NY 10014
www.nyrb.com

Library of Congress Cataloging-in-Publication Data

Sifton, Elisabeth, author.
  No ordinary men : Dietrich Bonhoeffer and Hans von Dohnanyi, resisters against Hitler in
church and state / by Elisabeth Sifton and Fritz Stern.
    pages cm. — (New York Review Books collections)
  Includes bibliographical references.
  ISBN 978-1-59017-681-8 (alk. paper)
  1. Bonhoeffer, Dietrich, 1906-1945. 2. Dohnanyi, Hans von, 1902-1945. 3. Anti-Nazi movement—Germany—Biography. 4. Government, Resistance to—Germany—History—20th
century. 5. Church and state—Germany—History—20th century. 6. Theologians—Germany—
Biography. 7. Lawyers—Germany—Biography. I. Stern, Fritz Richard, 1926- author. II. Title.
  BX4827.B57S57 2013
  943.086092'2—dc23
                                2013015555

ISBN 978-1-59017-681-8
Available as an electronic book; ISBN 978-1-59017-702-0

Printed in the United States of America on acid-free paper.

2 4 6 8 10 9 7 5 3 1

Contents

To the memory of our parents

Preface

HITLER'S THIRD REICH was the twentieth century's most popular tyranny: millions of jubilant Germans cheered while tens of thousands, then millions, and eventually much of the world suffered. His regime could boast of economic success rapidly achieved, of German power regained and German prestige restored—but then squandered in satanic barbarism. The Nazis' public pageantry always had terror in the wings, and we must understand the cunning with which they cajoled people into supporting their actions while at the same time intimidating them through terror, torture, and murder; it is an object lesson in the use of power for evil ends.

To oppose such a regime was rare and fraught with danger. To do so in order to protect the sanctity of law and of faith was rarer still. We are concerned in this book with the lives and actions of two admirable men who from the start of the Third Reich did their utmost, each in his own way, to oppose Nazi outrages, and who then conspired to overthrow the tyrant. One, Hans von Dohnanyi, a lawyer, is scarcely known in the United States; the other, his brother-in-law Dietrich Bonhoeffer, a pastor, has become very well known; there is also Christine—Dietrich's sister and Hans's wife.

On April 5, 1943, the Gestapo arrested all three: the brave and gifted lawyer who as an important member of the army's counterintelligence section had become a major figure in the civilian branch of the conspiracy against Hitler; the forceful, dedicated young pastor who for a decade had been battling Nazi racial thought and action in Germany's Protestant churches, which were largely bereft of principled opponents to Hitler's godless tyranny; and the woman who all along assisted her husband and brother. The three were united in a bond of decency and courage that was itself the rock on which resistance to tyranny could be built. Christine was released within the month, but the men were never freed. After two years in jail under terrible conditions and subjected to humiliating interrogations, Bonhoeffer and Dohnanyi were murdered, on Hitler's express orders, in April 1945, just weeks before the Führer's suicide and Germany's surrender.

After the war, Eberhard Bethge, a friend and student of Bonhoeffer's who became his literary executor, published some of the letters Bonhoeffer had written from jail, mostly letters to Bethge about the theological and ethical thoughts he had pondered while behind bars. When *Letters and Papers from Prison* appeared in 1951, it aroused great interest, and Bethge began work on a biography, which was published in 1967. A stream of commentary, analysis, dramatic presentations, films, and new material by and about Bonhoeffer has flowed on ever since. Dohnanyi appears in some of these sources, as do other family members, but Bonhoeffer is of course at the center.*

At the same time, scholars and writers have closely scrutinized the historical record of Germany during the Nazi period: a large number of Holocaust studies treat *that* subject down to every last numbing murderous detail, while a smaller, less noticed, but respectable body of literature focuses on the German resistance—a subject that was

---

*For more on Bethge's work, see the Appendix.

scarcely thought to have existed when *Letters and Papers from Prison* first came out. What emerges are two almost separate worlds, but the significant links between them have gone largely unobserved, and they are dramatically visible in the story of Dohnanyi, Bonhoeffer, and their allies. For among those opposed from the start to Hitler's rule—appalled by its violations of law, precedent, and decency —it was increasing outrage about the Nazi atrocities against Jews that became a major motive for the decision to resist Hitler and ultimately to try to remove him. The conspirators knew unspeakable truths about what was happening in Germany that many people not only in Germany but also in the outside world did not know and did not want to know. And they were ready and willing to take action against the regime.

These resisters were not necessarily friends of the Jews. It is doubtful that many of them were. Some of them may have had residues of Christian prejudice, or feelings that ranged from reserve to repulsion about Jews generally and about Germany's prosperous, highly ambitious Jews in particular; such feelings ran strong among some Jews themselves and many gentiles elsewhere in the West as well. However, to see the state discriminate against Jews, to see the beginnings of enforced pariahdom and worse—this prompted sympathetic support for Jews among many members of the Bonhoeffer circle. They understood instinctively that Jews were being robbed of their dignity, then of their very existence in a barbaric outrage that ended in a catastrophe not seen in Europe since the Thirty Years' War. For many, the organized bestiality was also an outrage against God, one that would be a burden of guilt for their countrymen forever.

In any account of Bonhoeffer and Dohnanyi, we should remember to keep two general points in mind. The members of the Bonhoeffer family—Dietrich's father, Dr. Karl Bonhoeffer, Germany's preeminent psychiatrist; his mother, Paula (née von Hase), daughter and granddaughter of aristocrats and well-known clerics; Dietrich; and his siblings—were remarkable examples of devotion and closeness to one another; they embodied certain virtues that they rarely mentioned but sturdily demonstrated: decency and hard work, reasonable selflessness, responsibility for others, and unexcelled courage. And throughout the upheavals of 1914–1945, the Bonhoeffers responded to the horrors convulsing Germany and Europe in a manner that was radically and honorably different from that chosen by the vast majority of Germans. Most members of the high professional elite to which they belonged either succumbed to the temptation of National Socialism—perhaps regretting some "excesses," perhaps impressed by the Nazis' pseudo-religious rhetoric—or clung to the illusion that in the Third Reich one could be "unpolitical," playing it safe or going into "inner emigration."

In the course of our exploration of the lives and work of these two men, we have come to understand Dohnanyi's centrality in their efforts, as well as the exceptional closeness between him and his brother-in-law. Resistance during Germany's darkest time was a larger, deeper, and more complicated drama than is usually depicted, and we have tried to reconstruct at least something of it here.

In the interest of full disclosure: Elisabeth's father, Reinhold Niebuhr, taught Dietrich Bonhoeffer in 1930–1931 and was thereafter something of a long-distance mentor to him; he also taught Bonhoeffer's cousin Hans Christoph von Hase, and he and his wife, also a theologian, stayed in touch with many members of the family for decades. As Bonhoeffer knew, Niebuhr was devoted to and active in the international ecumenical movement and had a special concern for the travails of German Protestantism. Fritz's parents and grandparents were friends and colleagues of Dr. Karl Bonhoeffer and friends, too, of some of the younger generation, especially Karl-Friedrich. Fritz has been since the 1960s a friend and colleague of the historian Karl-Dietrich Bracher, whose wife, Dorothee, is a daughter of Dietrich's sister Ursula Bonhoeffer and the murdered Rüdiger Schleicher. Both authors are friends of Klaus von Dohnanyi, son of Hans.

This book began with a commission from Robert Silvers to review new books about Dietrich Bonhoeffer for *The New York Review of Books*. Our decision to amplify our work came as we realized how much bigger the story was than Bonhoeffer's alone; we present it here knowing that it is but a small contribution to a much larger history.

I

IN 1912 KARL and Paula Bonhoeffer arrived in Berlin from Breslau, in eastern Germany (now Wrocław, in Poland), where Karl had begun his outstanding career on the celebrated medical faculty at Breslau University, and where Paula had grown up. Karl was descended from a patrician family in Württemberg; his forefathers were doctors and lawyers and his mother, Julie Tafel Bonhoeffer, was an energetic early feminist from a family noted for its freewheeling liberal, even revolutionary opinions. He had Swabian characteristics—a certain reserve, a rather un-Prussian serenity—and when he met the somewhat younger Paula von Hase she made what he called an "almost mystical" impression on him.[1]* His first position in Breslau had been on the medical staff of a clinic for insane prisoners; his new appointment, in 1912, as head of neurology and psychiatry at the Charité, Berlin's principal hospital, put him at the pinnacle of the German psychiatric profession.

The Bonhoeffers had eight healthy children, four girls and four boys, when they moved four years later to Grunewald, the pleasant,

---

*Numbered source notes are at the back of the book, beginning on page 151.

leafy district of Berlin that was popular with the capital's upper classes. They lived austerely, in Spartan luxury, in a comfortable big house with a big garden (chosen so that they could keep goats and chickens—useful at times of scarcity during the Great War). The children's uncle Hans von Hase lived in a rectory nearby, as did their maternal grandfather, the well-known theologian Karl-Alfred von Hase. Other neighbors and colleagues included the historian and theologian Adolf von Harnack and his family; the physicist and Nobel laureate Max Planck and his family; Planck's brother-in-law the renowned historian Hans Delbrück, with his seven children, among them Justus, Emilie, and Max (a Nobel laureate-to-be); and the museum director Richard Schöne, who was next door. There was also a significant presence of highly assimilated Jews—some of them friends of the family.

Their resourceful and greatly respected mother homeschooled the Bonhoeffer children until they were seven or eight (her observation that "Germans have their backbones broken twice in life: first in the schools, second in the military" became a family truism), and they excelled at their gymnasia and universities. All of them were good at sports (their father taught them tennis and skating) and music (their Hase grandmother had been a student of Clara Schumann's). The children regularly played and sang together; music heard or remembered was always with them. (Emmi Delbrück Bonhoeffer recalled much later that during the Nazi years the family's musical evenings also became "the camouflage for many conspiratorial meetings."[2]) This high-spirited, enviably talented family was privileged and they knew it, but modesty and a full awareness of how others lived were among their virtues. And Dr. Bonhoeffer was the living example of the physician's ethos, with his dedication to his patients and his devotion to clinical work and research.

In 1914, with the outbreak of the Great War, most of the elite of

Germany's clergy and professoriat thrilled to what they saw as a challenge to the nation, a moral trial for Germany that would purge it of its all-consuming materialism. The Bonhoeffers too were proud of their country and hopeful about its future, but as the horrors of the war continued so remorselessly over the next three years, they shrank from the nationalist superpatriots who clamored for a victory that would ensure Germany's invincible supremacy in Europe.* They learned of the deaths of cherished cousins, of terrible, mutilating wounds; the parents began to fear for their oldest sons, who by 1917 would be nineteen, eighteen, and sixteen—and subject to call-up. Indeed in 1917 the two oldest enlisted in the infantry and were sent to the front; in April 1918 the second son, Walter, died of wounds incurred in Germany's last great spring offensive. A letter that he

---

*At this time Dr. Bonhoeffer was drawn into a fierce controversy about the etiology of what Germans came to call "traumatic neurosis" (there being no German equivalent in word or thought for "shell shock"). True to his empirical methods and based on his own clinical observations near Verdun in 1916 where he visited German hospitals and Allied prisoner-of-war camps, he concluded that the symptoms among the wounded German soldiers were hysterical, brought on by fears of returning to the front; Allied prisoners of war did not seem to have these fears or symptoms. This fit into his general view that will was a decisive force in shaping conduct. And he seems to have been opposed to the crude and painful electric shock treatment then being developed, which the German army command favored as expediting the quick return of soldiers to the front.

Long after, he recalled a telling wartime incident: he had met with Emil Kraepelin, the founder of German psychiatry, with whom he spent almost a day talking about alcoholism; he noted Kraepelin's "fanatical faith," which he similarly found expressed when Kraepelin "tried to convince me that [Germany's] unrestricted submarine warfare signified a certain guarantee of victory"—evidence that Bonhoeffer was a "moderate" opposing unrestricted submarine warfare. See Zutt et al., *Karl Bonhoeffer*, pp. 67 and 87–94; see also Karl Bonhoeffer, "Vergleichende psychopathologische Erfahrungen aus den beiden Weltkriegen," *Der Nervenarzt*, Vol. 18, No. 1 (January 1, 1947)—the journal's first issue since July–September 1944—and Uwe Gerrens, *Medizinisches Ethos und theologische Ethik: Karl und Dietrich Bonhoeffer in der Auseinandersetzung um Zwangssterilisation und "Euthanasie" im Nationalsozialismus* (Munich: Oldenbourg, 1996), pp. 57–63.

wrote from a field hospital just hours before his death shows the characteristic Bonhoeffer strength:

My technique of not thinking about pain had to serve here too. But there are more interesting things in the world at present than my wound . . . and today's news of the taking of Ypres gives us great cause for hope. I dare not think about my poor regiment, so hard were the past few days for it. How are things going with the other officer cadets? I think of all of you with longing, my dears, every minute of the long days and nights.[3]

Dietrich's twin sister, Sabine, remembered "the terrible shadow that suddenly blotted out for us" what had been a "bright morning in May" when their vigorous, unflappable father turned white as he opened the telegram envelopes—one message telling of Walter's hospitalization, the second of his death—and sank into a chair "where he sat bowed over it with his head resting on his arms, his face hidden in his hands." When Dr. Bonhoeffer roused himself to tell the news to his wife, he grimly clutched the banister "as he went up the broad, easy staircase which at other times he mounted so lightly." The parents stayed alone together for hours.

The death of Walter and, within months, the wounding of the oldest brother, Karl-Friedrich, and the call-up of the younger Klaus devastated Mrs. Bonhoeffer, who withdrew to a darkened bedroom in the Schönes' house for weeks. Yet it was she who chose the recessional hymn at Walter's funeral, the familiar, beautiful chorale "What God has done, it is well done. / His will is always just."

By early 1918, America had entered the war and Russia—exhausted and under Bolshevik rule—had left it. The hapless Kaiser Wilhelm yielded all effective power to a concealed military dictatorship, which in turn helped to sponsor a rapidly growing antidemocratic movement, the Fatherland Party. A group of distinguished "moderates"—among them Hans Delbrück, Max Planck, Max Weber, Adolf von Harnack, and Ernst Troeltsch—had also emerged, renouncing their earlier enthusiasm for the war, pressing for an end to the slaughter, advocating domestic reforms that would help to reduce Germany's blatant political inequalities, and demanding a negotiated peace. The Fatherland Party reactionaries scorned these proposals for reform, rejected efforts to seek reasonable peace terms, and assailed their opponents (whom they vilified as principally Marxists and Jews) as weaklings. "The dead should not have died in vain," cried the super-patriots, while additional tens of thousands perished on the battlefield. The unity of 1914 disintegrated, and distrust of their leaders began to divide the German people.

On the day of the harsh armistice in November 1918, the great church historian and theologian Ernst Troeltsch wrote of the war's unexpected end: "At least the killing has ended, the illusion is gone, and the system has collapsed under its own sin." (It was largely left to Troeltsch and Thomas Mann, both of whom had once extolled the Spirit of 1914, to be the public voices warning against the growing influence of radical right-wing demagogy; since they themselves had once succumbed to it, they knew its attractions.) The two Bonhoeffer boys came home from the front somewhat radicalized; Karl-Friedrich was prepared to accept the revolution that toppled the old order and briefly brought Socialists into power.

Their father, on the other hand, was shocked by what he saw of the 1918 revolution, concluding that psychopaths had a prominent part in it. In retrospect he emphasized his worry then that the wartime deaths of a million soldiers between the ages of nineteen and twenty-nine had eliminated "socially and biologically valuable men" and increased the prevalence of "inferior" ones. His argument at least should have put paid to the German myth, so strong in 1914, that wars favor a kind of selection of the fittest. No, he believed, on the contrary the war might have furthered Germany's moral and physical enfeeblement—a train of thought that left him receptive to ideas about eugenics, then generally popular, especially in the United States.[4]

That the Great War was the Ur-catastrophe of the twentieth century has become common wisdom in our time; for Dr. Bonhoeffer it was probably his formative political experience, the first occasion, for him—as for many Germans—when public events shook and overwhelmed private lives. Every aspect of his life was affected—the private, the professional, the patriotic—and it prefigured his far crueler experience in the Second World War. Perhaps it strengthened his moral and social conservatism, though politically he was loyal to the Republic. As we shall see, his political and professional antennae were sensitively attuned to the emergence of psychopathic leaders in times of upheaval. He did not become a political person, but in a distant and professional manner he understood the psychic dramas of the post-1918 world.

During the Nazi years, at moments when outside cruelties threatened inner life and expectations, all the Bonhoeffers would recall Walter's death. For Dr. Bonhoeffer, very much the benign, traditional paterfamilias, a clinical concern for psychic health and an utter rootedness in his family seem to have sustained his courage, vision, and serenity.

Most Germans were stunned by their nation's sudden defeat in 1918, the road to it having been so well hidden by wartime censorship, and many mourned the disappearance of ancient monarchies and dynasties; they considered the Weimar Republic with its revolutionary trappings as a strange, alien excrescence on the body of their nation. The questions "Who lost the war?" and then "Who accepted the ignominious peace of Versailles?" were dominant. Hitler's answer—that Jews and Marxists had—was a basic tenet of his unceasing propaganda in the 1920s, and it appealed to Germans as an escape from the truth. Also, virtually all Germans were outraged by the harsh terms of the Versailles Treaty (as were some non-Germans, notably John Maynard Keynes): the right seethed in resentment of President Wilson's "betrayal," moderates despised the treaty yet were prepared to work for its gradual revision, and everyone was indignant about the "war-guilt" clause, which made Germany "solely" responsible for the outbreak of the war.*

The Bonhoeffers felt the tension of these conflicts, and they also understood another calamitous feature of the times, which concerned religion. Weimar's constitution had brought the traditional alliance between throne and Protestant altar to something of an end with its careful, modest redefinition of church–state relations. Germany's Protestant churches—*Landeskirchen* that for almost four centuries had enjoyed the reigning powers' protection and support in the various duchies, kingdoms, and cities that made up Germany before its unification in 1871—were now uncertain of their legal and financial future, and they also were devastated by Germany's defeat, having believed that the Spirit of 1914 perfectly expressed their German Protestant faith. Most church leaders, horrified by the events of 1918,

---

*Zara Steiner, a distinguished British historian, has recently concluded, "The Versailles treaty did not solve the German problem, but the traditional view that it was a Carthaginian peace needs to be abandoned." See *The Lights That Failed: European International History 1919–1933* (Oxford University Press, 2005), p. 606.

felt "homeless," as Klaus Scholder has put it,* so it is not surprising that much of the Protestant establishment was suspicious of, and hostile toward, the Weimar Republic.

In truth the Protestant churches had already lost moral strength before 1914, all too often functioning as mere decorative shells for pious but secular bourgeois life; a few outspoken Christians had themselves said as much. When in 1924, at the age of eighteen, Dietrich Bonhoeffer went on his first trip to Italy with his brother Klaus and witnessed the vibrant energy of a religious culture completely different from his own, he mused that perhaps in Germany the Protestant churches' eagerness to be officially established had over the centuries drained them of vital meaning, that "the more political circumstances changed, the more it lost its hold over the people, until finally the term 'Protestantism' concealed a great deal that, frankly and honestly, was nothing but materialism...for too long it has been a refuge for homeless spirits, a shelter for uneducated enlightenment."[5]

Pastors concerned about the moral ill health of the churches, about their far-reaching secularization and the alienation of the growing proletariat from them—conditions that had worsened during the war—had to deal with the old-fashioned conservative clerics who

---

*See his excellent *The Churches and the Third Reich, Vol. 1: Preliminary History and the Time of Illusions, 1918–1934* (Fortress, 1988), p. 3. The governance of Protestant churches in Germany displayed confusing, sometimes discordant elements due to their having evolved when Germany was still a congeries of small principalities and large states. Most communities had either a Lutheran, a Calvinist, or a Catholic majority, but the decisive factor was usually the professed faith of the ruler. However, Prussia's Calvinist rulers, the Hohenzollerns, reigned over mostly Lutheran subjects; in the seventeenth century this had been thought to promote tolerance; in the nineteenth century, Prussia succeeded in creating a Calvinist and Lutheran fusion called the Church of the Prussian Union, but that didn't cover all of Germany. For legal, doctrinal, sectarian, or fiercely local reasons the *Landeskirchen* were a jumble of entities. This made it both easier and harder for the Nazis to attack them.

greatly outnumbered them; among these were activists who wanted a "league" of *Landeskirchen* to band together with the goal of emphasizing the essential Germanness of Protestantism. (They had made a big point of this in 1917, the quatercentenary of Luther nailing his ninety-five theses to the door of the Castle Church in Wittenberg.) These "German Christians," as they called themselves, were keen to emphasize the Nordic roots of German faith and wanted to downplay or eliminate the Old Testament in Protestant theology. The anti-Semitism that had marked so much of German Christendom before 1914 now became far more virulent, and it mixed with seething resentments of "Weimar modernity." This bigotry sullied much of the German Evangelical Church—the federation created in 1924 of Germany's independent Lutheran, Calvinist, United, and Reformed Protestant parishes.

The Bonhoeffers were appalled by the ferocious mendacity and physical violence of right-wing nationalistic thugs and early Nazis. And they were outraged by the murder in Berlin in 1922 of Weimar's foreign minister, the Jewish industrialist and statesman Walther Rathenau, who was gunned down as he was driven to work from his home in Grunewald. They rightly—and instantly—saw this crime as a portent. Dietrich reported to Sabine on June 25 that the day before, he and his classmates had heard in school "a strange crackling. It was the murder of Rathenau—only 300 meters from us. Swinish types [*Schweinevolk*] of rightist Bolsheviks [*Rechtsbolschewisten*]." (Dietrich rightly intuited an affinity of radical right-wing murderers and Bolsheviks.[6] A year later, Karl Radek, a leading Comintern member, floated the idea of some kind of collaboration between Bolsheviks and right-wing German nationalists.) Christine wrote to her fiancé, Hans von Dohnanyi, then a law student in Berlin, that "of all the hideous acts of these accursed swastika people," this was the worst yet.[7] He did not disagree. Rathenau's assassination signaled that Germany's government was in serious danger, he told her on July 1. "The police have brought to light huge whole lists of [more] marked targets for murder."[8] Another letter to Dohnanyi, this one from Christine's brother Klaus, reported on further sickening displays of loutish political behavior among his fellow law students: "Hans, only think of the trouble we shall have later with these people."[9]

Dietrich, who matriculated the next year at the University of Tübingen (following his brothers and sisters in starting out at their father's Swabian alma mater), appreciated that this milestone in his young life was occurring at an extraordinary time, when Germany was being ravaged by the great inflation that caused its currency to lose value by the day, and when the integrity of the Weimar Republic was being threatened by separatist elements and by violent political uprisings on the left and the right. He reported to his parents that he had to spend a billion marks for each meal and six billion for bread.

More important, he told them about his activities in Tübingen's Hedgehog fraternity—to which his father and uncles had belonged, though not his older brothers. In the autumn of 1923 as a Hedgehog member he received two weeks of military training in Ulm under Reichswehr officers, thanks to a program set up by the Württemberg state government to have forces ready in case of a general strike; Hedgehog men had already been used to help quell uprisings in Stuttgart and Munich in 1919, which is why Karl-Friedrich and Klaus had refused to join. He weighed the pros and cons and received guarded approval not only from his parents but from his grandmother Julie Tafel Bonhoeffer, who lived in Tübingen—an energetic, fearless lady with outspokenly liberal political views. Dietrich appreciated the communitarian spirit of the fraternity while being sensibly immune to reactionary fervors.

Given the family's general tone, it was no surprise that they were all alarmed by Hitler's political successes. "From the start," Dr. Bonhoeffer wrote later, "we regarded the victory of National Socialism in 1933 and Hitler's appointment as Reich chancellor as a misfortune—the entire family agreed on this. In my own case, I disliked and distrusted Hitler because of his demagogic propagandistic speeches, his sympathy-telegram after the murder,*...[and] because of what I heard from professional colleagues about his psychopathic symptoms."[10]

In 1924 the eighteen-year-old Sabine told her parents that she was engaged to Gerhard (Gert) Leibholz, a converted Jew four years her senior with a promising career in law and state service. (Gert had met Klaus Bonhoeffer and Hans von Dohnanyi years before, when, as boys, all three were being prepared for confirmation.) Too young to have been drafted in the war, in 1918 he had volunteered for the Grenzschutz Ost, a paramilitary group that—like other Free Corps units that had sprung up after the war in violation of the Versailles Treaty—specialized in fighting the "Bolshevik danger" near the Polish border, but he only had a three-month course of basic training in Berlin. Soon he was studying law and showing himself loyal to the new Weimar Republic, even as its fervent right-wing critic the jurist and political philosopher Carl Schmitt thought highly of him as "a rising star in the judicial firmament" and met with him frequently in the late 1920s.[11]

Bonhoeffer family tradition forbade the children to marry before they were twenty, so Sabine's parents wanted her to wait; they also warned her that she would surely suffer from the discrimination Gert

---

*In the fall of 1932, five SA men were arrested for murdering a Communist in Potempa, in Upper Silesia, and when they were convicted Hitler cabled them his unconditional support. The convicted men were sentenced to death; on appeal the sentence was commuted to life imprisonment; when he came to power, Hitler freed all imprisoned Nazis in an amnesty.

would likely encounter in seeking advancement. Dr. Bonhoeffer noted that for years he had tried to get a full professorship for a distinguished colleague who was a converted Jew, and had not succeeded.* Some in the Bonhoeffers' extended family may have felt unease about having this somewhat Semitic young man in the clan. Their mother's brother-in-law Rüdiger Count von der Goltz, a Reichswehr general, refused to come to the wedding because, he said, his anti-Semitic beliefs made it impossible for him to acknowledge a Jew in the family. Christine dismissed him as an "Ass!"[12] Sabine and Gert married, and although he was appointed to a full professorship of legal studies at Greifswald in 1929, when he was only twenty-eight, the predicted difficulties soon ensued.

It had been something of a surprise to his family when Dietrich at the age of fourteen, in 1920, had proclaimed his intention to become a pastor. But perhaps it might have been anticipated. During the traumatic years 1917–1918, he and Sabine had developed a habit of intense bedtime meditations on the meaning of "eternity" and the promise of eternal life, and these may in some sense have prepared him. There was also the sway of his mother's family—after all, his Hase great-grandfather, grandfather, and uncle were all pastors. And

---

*In the Wilhelmine and then the Weimar years, a person of Jewish descent who had converted to (usually Protestant) Christianity had a somewhat easier time winning acceptance than an unconverted one. The brilliant art historian Richard Krautheimer tells of an unexpected experience when, as a young scholar in the 1920s, he asked a senior professor to sponsor his *Habilitation* (a further dissertation that was a prerequisite for an academic career). "By the way, are you still a Jew?" asked the older man. "Yes, Herr Geheimrat." "But that could be changed?" "No, Herr Geheimrat." And that was the end. He offered this story, Krautheimer says, "as a contribution to the portrait of Wilhelmine Germany within the Weimar Republic." And, he rightly adds, "The worst part of it was the naive innocence with which the suggestion was made." Richard Krautheimer, *Ausgewählte Aufsätze zur Europäischen Kunstgeschichte* (Cologne: DuMont, 1988), p. 11.

might not Dietrich have been affected by the spiritual turmoil of the postwar years and attracted to a life of service in a time of such moral uncertainty?

On the other hand the Bonhoeffers didn't often go to church; it was typical of upper-class German Protestants to attend baptisms, confirmations, weddings, and funerals, other occasions being optional. Still, their genuinely devout mother gave the children the equivalent of Sunday school lessons at home, and they observed devout customs: grace before meals, evening prayers before bedtime, large family celebrations at Christmas and Easter with Bible readings and hymns presided over by the agnostic father, whose generous respect for the practice of a faith he did not share demonstrated both natural courtesy and a benevolent recognition of the mysteries of the human heart. The parents did not talk about pastors or bishops, indeed rather dismissed them, and his older brothers scorned Dietrich's wish to be part of what they considered a weak, boring, petit bourgeois institution.[13] His recent biographers follow Eberhard Bethge in stressing Dietrich's yearning for independence, for a world beyond the here and now, and his evidently genuine aptitude and preference for the spiritual life carried the day. On his confirmation, his mother gave him the Bible that had once been Walter's; his decision, once taken, was not challenged or criticized by his parents or anyone else.

To assess the intellectual depth and mastery of Dietrich's university studies, we must first grasp how much knowledge, superficial or deep, was imparted to students in a good German gymnasium ninety years ago. When he went off to Tübingen, he had already learned Hebrew as well as Latin and Greek, was already reading in, and thinking about, Kant and Hegel, Ranke and Schleiermacher, Hesse and Ibsen, Catullus and Plotinus. He plunged into university studies with a well-trained, well-stocked mind and a well-developed appetite for learning.

Tübingen had long been respected for its theological excellence, but it wasn't, in 1923, where the intellectual excitement was. That was in Berlin, and Bonhoeffer transferred a year later to Berlin University. Its preeminence in what was considered liberal, positivist theology—meaning Christian doctrine expounded by rational scholars who submitted the sacred texts to strict scrutiny—had begun at its founding, in 1810, with its first theology professor, Friedrich Schleiermacher, who was known for the often controversial ways in which he brought Kantian and Enlightenment ideas about reason and experience, as well as early Romantic notions about the wellsprings of the spirit, to the interpretation of Christian scripture and dogma. By the twentieth century, two controversial church scholars, Adolf von Harnack and Ernst Troeltsch, had brought new renown to Berlin University, though neither of them was on the theology faculty.

Harnack, already a major figure in imperial Germany, had very broad intellectual interests, with administrative accomplishments as numerous as scholarly ones. This ambitious, ferociously hardworking professor was simultaneously director, beginning in 1905, of the Royal Library (after 1918 the Prussian State Library) and a founder and the first president, in 1911, of the Kaiser Wilhelm Gesellschaft (renamed the Max Planck Society after 1945); he also helped to draft sections of the Weimar Constitution relating to the church and education.

Harnack's magisterial, multivolume *History of Dogma*, published in the 1880s, had made his reputation as a scholar and "scientist" of the first order, with its meticulous study of the scriptural, periscriptural, Greek philosophical, and ecclesiastical sources of Christian doctrine, its rigorous methodology, and its fluent, expressive prose. Conservative Protestant authorities found him nearly blasphemous, however, notably in his dissection of the Apostles' Creed and his evenhanded demonstration of weaknesses in Luther's theology. Today, any reasonable reader can still appreciate the vigor and clarity of

Harnack's answers to the question "What is Christianity?"—the title of a famous small book he wrote in 1900.

By the time Bonhoeffer was studying theology in Berlin, Harnack was semiretired but still teaching a few courses. Bonhoeffer took his seminar on church history, which he found thrilling, and in honor of Harnack's seventy-fifth birthday in 1926 he organized with his fellow students a *Festschrift* on the subject of *chara* (joy) as treated in the New Testament and by the early church fathers—an excellent choice of subject, given Harnack's mastery of patristics. Harnack thought highly of his student, and marked his work "very good."

In some biographies of Bonhoeffer, Troeltsch doesn't figure much in his life or thought—one omits him entirely—but this is misleading. True, Bonhoeffer couldn't have studied with him, since Troeltsch's career in Berlin was cut short by his sudden death in 1923, but he had been a powerful, appealing figure in the capital's political and intellectual life, and the views he expressed in his running commentaries in the press on the fragility of Weimar and on its dangerous right-wing enemies had chimed in with the views of the Bonhoeffer family.

Troeltsch upset church conservatives even more than Harnack did, with his ebullient, engagé presence and masterful scholarship, which ranged well beyond theology. He stood firm in his insistence on studying Christianity in the context of the histories of religion and culture; in his learned demonstration that while the Reformation was indeed the beginning of the modern age in Europe, certain medieval, unmodern forms of belief persisted in Lutheranism; in his unprecedented study of the compromises made in the formation of Christian moral and social doctrines; even in his belief that European civilization could no longer be called Christian after the late eighteenth century. Moreover, he believed in the Christian commitment to social justice—then as now a controversial topic.

Bonhoeffer read Troeltsch's masterpiece *The Social Teachings of*

the Christian Churches (1912) at the for him advanced age of nineteen, in 1924–1925, when at the urging of his brother Klaus he also
began to read Max Weber, Troeltsch's friend. He was very taken with
their bold and provocative analyses of historical and contemporary
problems of church and society. He included Troeltsch in the first
lectures he gave as a fledgling instructor in Berlin in 1931–1932 on
the subject of twentieth-century theology, but by then he had fallen
under the spell of the contrarian, equally magisterial, Swiss theologian Karl Barth.

We know from Bonhoeffer's writings that he often put himself into
a torment when making life decisions, uncertain as he was of the
sources and motives for making them. Not that he was indecisive, but
he was always aware of the fallibility of one's mental processes. (He
was also, admirably, unafraid of his own anguished self-reproaches
and self-corrections.) One difficult early choice was whether to continue studying Christianity in its historical and social aspects in the
manner of Harnack and Troeltsch or to focus on theology as Barth
taught it, emphasizing the radical transcendence of God as the
"wholly other," insisting that God as revealed in the crucifixion of
Jesus cannot and must not be assimilated to any specific human culture or achievement. This was not an obscure or arcane matter: Barth's
challenge to Harnack and Troeltsch—set forth in his *Epistle to the
Romans*, published in 1919—was still rocking the theological world.*

---

*Barth, too, had studied with Harnack. He was shocked when his revered teacher signed
the notorious "Manifesto of the Ninety-three" of October 1914, in which some of Germany's most prestigious writers, scholars, and scientists declared that the Allies' accusa-
tions about German atrocities were false, insisted on Germany's innocence in a war that
had been forced on it, and praised Germany's military power for being the indispensable
protector of German culture. Barth thought Harnack had been misled by his "liberal"
theology, which tied divine purpose too closely to human actions, and was appalled by the
terrible mistake of claiming divine support for the nation's cause, an error committed
perhaps even more brazenly in Germany than in the Allied countries.

Bonhoeffer was enthralled by Barth's interpretation of the Gospels, and by his great theme: that above all Christians must heed, in their hearts, the "unbelievable, incredible, and certainly disturbing testimony that God himself said and did something; something entirely new, outside the correlation of all human words and things." Some students found Barth gloomy, but Bonhoeffer didn't, and he welcomed Barth's argument that the spiritual certainty sought by struggling believers, the true religious experience, "was anchored not in people but in the majesty of God."[14]

Yet he didn't go to study with Barth, and Harnack wasn't his principal adviser in Berlin; he warily carved out a thesis subject that went down the middle: "*Communio Sanctorum*: A Dogmatic Inquiry into the Sociology of the Church." This precocious, still very young student seemed to want somehow to resolve the celebrated dispute between Barth on the one hand and Harnack and Troeltsch on the other, which shows audacious confidence in his own intellectual capacities, and also why so many readers across the theological spectrum still find him appealing. In this early work, he did his best to offer a firm sociological explanation of what the church, or *a* church, actually is for its members and leaders—what defines it historically as a "living community"; and also a firm dogmatic (and Barthian) understanding of the Christian theology of revelation. His fellow divinity student and cousin Hans Christoph von Hase warned him that few would understand it: "the Barthians won't because of the sociology, and the sociologists won't because of Barth."[15]

By 1927 Bonhoeffer had finished his dissertation and was preparing for ordination, which could not happen until he was twenty-five (in 1931). At the recommendation of his church supervisor, he spent 1928 in Barcelona as a pastor at the German church there; then, after two years of teaching at Berlin University, he obtained a fellowship to study in the United States.

As soon as Bonhoeffer arrived in New York City, where he was to spend the 1930–1931 academic year at Union Theological Seminary, he could see the severe effects of what came to be called the Great Depression: unemployment in America as in Germany was the great scourge. President Herbert Hoover, like Chancellor Heinrich Brüning, had laissez-faire ideas about state nonintervention in the economy, however, and political discontent was mounting. Bonhoeffer may not have yet grasped how gravely the absence of strong political leadership affected both countries. And German politics changed for the worse after the September 1930 election, in which the Nazis dramatically increased their strength in the Reichstag, becoming its second-largest party. Dietrich's parents and his brother Klaus reported to him that the Nazis were successfully exploiting the economic crisis and convincing people that the Great Depression was due to failures of democracy; "people are flirting with fascism," as Klaus put it.[16] In America, on the other hand, Dietrich met quite a few students and church people who were demanding more active social and economic policies from the national administration, which came with the New Deal two years later.

Bonhoeffer enthusiasts have written often about the year when he studied at Union Theological Seminary principally because they are so taken with his discovery of the Abyssinian Baptist Church in Harlem (not far from Union), his enthusiastic respect for its style of worship, and his recognition of white Americans' racism, which did indeed shock him. His appreciation of the black American Baptist churches is certainly an important facet of his biography, as are his visits to Cuba and Mexico during his year in America. One of his most attractive qualities was his eagerness to experience living, vital religious practices wherever he found them.

It has puzzled some American scholars that while Bonhoeffer admired the sermons he heard at Abyssinian, he thought little of those preached by Union faculty members who were famous for their homiletic skills, notably Harry Emerson Fosdick and Reinhold Niebuhr, who were also renowned for their theological liberalism. Some evangelical fundamentalists of our time try to claim that these judgments, along with Bonhoeffer's snobbish dismissal of Union's curriculum, are evidence of his spiritual kinship with them, but this is nonsense. While he enjoyed introducing Barth's ideas to counter the theological liberals Harnack and Troeltsch, who were such strong influences on the Union professors, he hardly disavowed the German masters. Also, his training in biblical studies and theology, in European philosophy and history, was so far in advance of most Union students' work that intellectually he looked down on them *and* their teachers when it came to the core curriculum, where the virtual absence of exegesis and dogmatics offended him.

Yet Bonhoeffer realized—and the realization grew on him after he had returned to Europe—that the Union professors stressed genuinely important subjects for any pastoral student at the height of the Great Depression. He came to respect their emphasis on ethics, and recognized that his American classmates might be more alive than their German counterparts to the ethical challenges posed in ordinary political and social life. He was impressed that Union people were addressing the political and moral consequences of unemployment, for example—in 1930–1931 perhaps the most urgent issue in the world—and were willing to live and work among the disadvantaged.

Bonhoeffer also read and absorbed a fine variety of American books—among them Sinclair Lewis's devastating satirical portrait of a phony, opportunistic evangelical preacher, *Elmer Gantry*, and the novels of Theodore Dreiser; he found the philosophical works of William James "uncommonly fascinating." It took him years to digest and understand what he took on board in New York. More than a decade later, he thanked a senior church leader in Berlin for having helped him get to America for "a year that has been of the greatest importance to me ever since."[17]

Yet as some of his American friends noted, this still rather young student hadn't yet decided what he was going to do with all this learning, or how he would relate his theological and biblical studies to his sense of what it meant genuinely to practice the Christian faith. This truth came to him as he steadily matured in thought and in independence during the 1930s, and posthumously he is celebrated for the eloquence with which he expressed his credo. But he wasn't there yet.

When he returned to Germany in 1931 he couldn't settle down anymore than he had in America. His parents hoped he would join them, but instead he rushed off to Bonn to meet with Barth, stopping on his way in Frankfurt to see his brother Karl-Friedrich, who had just been made head of his own scientific institute, and who was especially eager for Dietrich to meet the newly born Karl Walter Paul Bonhoeffer.*

Bonhoeffer was entranced by Barth's personality at their first encounter and appreciated his openness in argument, yet Barth, who found the stranger on his doorstep interesting and well educated, was not at all sympathetic to Bonhoeffer's eagerness for instruction on the "problem of ethics, that is, the question of the possibility of [proclaiming] concrete commandments through the church."[18] Still, their discussions eventually blossomed into an enriching friendship for them both, and Bonhoeffer became devoted to him. Six months later he mentioned to Erwin Sutz, a Swiss friend he had met in America, that Barth's book *Saint Anselm's Proof of the Existence of God,* just published, was "a great delight to me," for it showed "those scholas-

---

*Karl-Friedrich mentioned that the baby "resembles you quite a bit and because of that you liked the picture of him." The big brother's teasing remark suggests the affectionate freedom within the family. *Dietrich Bonhoeffer Werke*, Vol. 11, p. 13.

tic cripples"* who doubted his capacities "that he really does know how to interpret and still remain sovereign." And he thanked Barth for having put up "with my perhaps too obstinate and—as you once said—'godless' questions."

Those "godless" questions concerned the "problem of ethics," which Barth considered secondary to and lesser than the ultimate question of what Christian belief rested on, the very question that Saint Anselm had struggled with. Bonhoeffer's stubbornness here shows not only the influence of what he had learned in America but his urgent sense that in the chaos of Germany at the time pastors must demonstrate, more clearly than they ever had before, on what basis they ministered to the people, and religious instruction must include ethical commands about what is valuable or meaningful in this sinful, suffering world.

He felt this all the more strongly when in 1931 he began teaching a confirmation class for several dozen boys in an impoverished working-class district of Berlin, along with becoming the chaplain for students at the Berlin Technical Institute (now the Technical University), where most of his flock came from wretched family circumstances. He could not, and did not want to, disregard the dangerous conditions that afflicted people all over Europe. In Germany public life was in an "unprecedented" state, he thought. Writing in October 1931 to Sutz, he reported that "the outlook is really exceptionally grim. There is in fact no one in Germany who can see ahead even a little way," even though people were sure they were "standing at a tremendous turning point in world history. Whether it will lead to Bolshevism or to a general reconciliation, who knows? And after all, who knows which is better? But the coming winter will leave no one

---

*His spirited neologism *Wissenschaftkrüppel* is enticing: scholars crippled by their faith in "scientific" learning. *Dietrich Bonhoeffer Werke*, Vol. 11, p. 51.

in Germany untouched. Seven million unemployed, fifteen or twenty million hungry—I don't know how Germany...will survive it." And what was the church to do? Bonhoeffer wondered. "Will our church survive *yet* another catastrophe [or] will that not really be the end unless we become something completely different? Speak, live completely differently? But how?...The omens are strange."[19] To another friend he suggested that perhaps rescue might come from some other large nation—he mentioned India. "Otherwise the last great agony of Christianity is upon us."

Bonhoeffer's friend and fellow pastor Franz Hildebrandt* shared his foreboding. And he, too, was concerned at a very deep level about the question that all young clergymen must face when first they mount the pulpit: On what authority do they give instruction and solace to vexed or frightened people? If they claim God's authority, how has it been transmitted to them? Hildebrandt reminded Bonhoeffer of the great biblical passage about Jehoshaphat, king of Judah, faced by a powerful coalition against him and praying to God for guidance: "We have no might against this great company that cometh against us; neither know we what to do; but our eyes are upon thee" (II Chronicles 20:12). There was no biblical text Bonhoeffer quoted in 1932 more than this one. It is often used to illustrate the virtues and strengths of humility (the king willingly owns up, in public, to his uncertainty) and piety (praying in public, he affirms that he will follow God's word). For Bonhoeffer and Hildebrandt a crucial passage comes when the king is reminded that the

---

*Hildebrandt and Bonhoeffer had been friends since their student days in Berlin; they shared a passion for music, an appetite for fierce debate on theological and ecclesiastical issues, and a prodigious capacity for hard work. In his pastoral tasks Hildebrandt put into practice some of the progressive ideas of Weimar reformers. See Holger Roggelin, *Franz Hildebrandt: Ein lutherischer Dissenter im Kirchenkampf und Exil* (Göttingen: Vandenhoeck & Ruprecht, 1999).

fate of Judah is not his to control, but God's; trust in the Lord will give him the strength needed to defeat its enemies.*

Equally important for Bonhoeffer was his eye-opening experience a few months later in England when he went, as a German "youth secretary," to a conference of a well-established group called the World Alliance for Promoting International Friendship Through the Churches; this was where he first encountered the forward-looking ecumenical figures who came to mean so much to him. Since the very beginning of the Great War, clerical and lay church leaders in the United States, England, and Europe had been working to get Protestants to cooperate across national and denominational lines, even to seek alliances with Catholic, Orthodox, Jewish, and secular groups, in the interests of promoting peace and resolving issues that led to war. The World Alliance aimed to organize so that, in its words, "the weight of all churches and Christians can be brought to bear upon the relations of governments and peoples...[so] that there may be substituted arbitration for war in the settlement of international disputes; friendship in place of suspicion and hate; co-operation instead of ruinous competition; and a spirit of service and sacrifice rather than that of greed and gain."

Bonhoeffer was attracted by the open-minded internationalism of the ecumenical movement,† and he became active in it, though like

---

* "Be not afraid nor dismayed by reason of this great multitude; for the battle is not yours, but God's ... see the salvation of the Lord with you, O Judah and Jerusalem ... tomorrow go out against them: for the Lord will be with you" (II Chronicles 20:15,17).

†The ecumenical movement, well organized in thirty countries, especially in Great Britain and the United States, brought people together across party-political lines, too, to discuss issues such as disarmament, the treatment of racial and religious minorities, conscientious objection, refugees, peace education, and arms control. In America, the then socialist Niebuhr and the Republicans John Foster Dulles and Charles Taft were active in it. Roman Catholics, like fundamentalist Protestant evangelicals, declined invitations to join the ecumenists—then, and for the next half-century or more.

most German scholars and scientists he found it repugnant to debate with counterparts from former Allied countries who hewed to the Versailles war-guilt clause, just as they found it repugnant to talk to Germans who didn't offer "a word of sympathy for our plundered and destroyed churches," as one French delegate put it, who "bewailed only the suffering of their own people, whose complete innocence they proclaimed."[20] He also thought that the World Alliance people, like his teachers and fellow students in New York, didn't have an adequate theological basis for their work. It was all very well to say that Christians' shared understanding of the New Testament should be couched in terms broad enough to encourage people to welcome the Gospel whether they were rich or poor, Jew or Greek, bond or free, male or female (to paraphrase the passage in the Epistle to the Galatians that ecumenists love to quote), but Bonhoeffer thought they ought first to sort out their varying conceptions of what "the kingdom of God" really meant. If they didn't know how to relate that imagined kingdom to the modern world's temporal kingdoms—if their theology was weak on this point—they would be defenseless against political or doctrinal attack.

Still, the World Alliance's eagerness to draw young people into its programs gave Bonhoeffer hope that the group's work would help to overcome the destructive divisions of the past. In fact his intense commitment to this ecumenical ideal did much to reenergize the movement. At the close of the conference, he was made one of three "international youth delegates," a position that enabled him to stay in touch with some of Protestantism's most active progressives, and they with him; the immense value of this connection would soon be apparent. And when the group met again in 1932 in Czechoslovakia, he reminded them that Germans of all persuasions still rejected the Versailles war-guilt clause; he warned that their "feeling of injustice and...their *völkische* consciousness are being exploited by extreme elements," and that the National Socialists were using democratic means to establish a dictatorship.[21] He inveighed against mere warnings about rearmament (a favorite theme of the ecumenists), pointing out that already the "demons are here."

He was ambitious and restless, a condition that became, or perhaps always was, characteristic, though in these formative years he was also suspicious of his own ambitions, finding them deeply un-Christian. In the next several years he fit half a dozen ecumenical trips to other countries in between his new obligations to lecture on theology at Berlin University* and to begin pastoral work at the Technical Institute; it wasn't clear to him or anyone else whether he would decide on an ecumenical, academic, or pastoral career. With the focused energy that was characteristic of his family, he plunged into all three. He was still in his twenties.

The other Bonhoeffer children were also forging ahead, with excellent appointments to good faculties or government posts. Also, by 1930 all but Dietrich were married—and to remarkable people, most of whom they had known since the sandbox, as Germans say. First his sister Ursula had married a lawyer, Rüdiger Schleicher, in 1924. Schleicher was a Swabian, like Dr. Bonhoeffer; he identified himself as a South German liberal. He had been severely wounded in the Great War, at the end of which he joined the newly founded German Democratic Party, a bourgeois pillar of the Weimar Republic. Sabine had become the wife of Gert Leibholz. The Bonhoeffers' lawyer son Klaus wed Emilie Delbrück, and two Bonhoeffers married children

---

*Partial reconstructions of his first year of lectures have been made from his own notes and from students' notes. They covered a fascinating, wide range of material—not only from the key German theologians of the first decades of the century but also from William James and Dostoyevsky—and he paid attention to the social and intellectual conditions that nourished these writers. The sheer breadth of the young man's erudition remains astounding.

of the Hungarian pianist and composer Ernst von Dohnányi*: the oldest son, the chemist Karl-Friedrich, to Grete von Dohnanyi, and Christine to Hans von Dohnanyi. The Bonhoeffer parents and these children of the second generation were to give indispensable moral and practical support to one another during the Hitler years when they were all in opposition; and when some of them moved on to active resistance, they were all well aware of the risks.

---

*Dohnányi lived and worked in Berlin from 1902 to 1915; he separated from his wife, the pianist Elisabeth Kunwald, in 1913 and eventually returned to Budapest; his two sons continued to live with their mother in Berlin. The war years were a difficult time for a single mother who earned her meager keep by giving music lessons (Hans at age fourteen was tutoring some of his classmates); one can imagine that the Bonhoeffer family must have seemed attractive and congenial to them. See Smid, *Hans von Dohnanyi, Christine Bonhoeffer*, pp. 16–18.

II

ON THE EVENING of January 30, 1933, after President Paul von Hindenburg named Hitler chancellor in a new government and the Nazis organized a huge torch-lit parade in Berlin to celebrate, Rüdiger Schleicher rushed home and announced, "This means war!"[22] And right he was—war at home and war abroad, though no one could have predicted the horror that Hitler and his regime would unleash upon the world. A week later Bonhoeffer wrote to his onetime American teacher Reinhold Niebuhr:

It would be precipitous to say even one word about the state of affairs here in Germany. It can scarcely be expected that nothing will substantially change here, whether economically, politically, or socially. But an even greater threat is a terrible barbarization of our culture....The Church's path is darker than it has ever been.... For the rest there is no denying that we—especially we in Europe—live in an uncannily interesting time and one would hardly want to wish to exchange it for another time.[23]

Perhaps Dietrich felt differently about the "interesting time" a few months later, after he had declined his twin sister Sabine's request that he preside over the burial of her Jewish (and unbaptized) father-in-law, who died on April 11, a refusal counseled by the church superior whose advice he had sought. It tormented him, and six months later he wrote to Gert and Sabine: "To be frank, I can't think what made me behave as I did. How could I have been so horribly afraid at the time?...It preys on my mind because it's the kind of thing one can never make up for."[24]

He had made a public accommodation that in short order offended his private decency—an inner dispute that became familiar to any German with a conscience. Karl Bonhoeffer experienced it, too: in his memoirs he recalled that he stopped attending official functions at the university after he had gone to a speech given there by Bernard Rust, an ardent Nazi who was Hitler's minister of science, education, and culture: "Considering Rust's offensive attitude toward the professoriat, it was unfortunate that neither I nor other professors had the courage to leave the auditorium."[25] Both father and son had succumbed to an insidious fear—a fear that afflicted many Germans—but they, unlike so many others, resolved not to give in again. And there was a fine model of fearlessness in their own family: when the Nazi Party organized a daylong boycott of Jewish establishments on April 1, 1933, Dr. Bonhoeffer's mother, then ninety-one, made a point of crossing the line of SA men (members of the Nazis' paramilitary Sturmabteilung—Assault Division) who had formed a cordon around the targeted department store Kaufhaus des Westens, in Berlin, and went shopping there. (The boycott was intended not only to intimidate Germans but also as a signal to the rest of the world that Germany's new government would hold German Jews hostage against any anti-German acts abroad.)

It was pure accident that only two days after Hitler's appointment as chancellor Dietrich found himself in front of a radio microphone for the only time in his life, broadcasting a speech (arranged weeks earlier) on the all too apt subject "The Younger Generation's Altered View of the Concept of *Führer.*" What had altered young Germany's idea of leadership? He rightly asserted that the defeat in 1918 had "made a latent crisis visible. Inwardly Germany broke apart." And, he argued, because of this social breakdown, young people—especially those inspired by the burgeoning German Youth Movement—clamored for an authoritative leader whose powers would derive from the intuitive, not the elective choice of his followers. If such a leader [*Führer*] forgot the true source of his power or violated the principles of state rectitude, Dietrich went on, "he stands in danger of becoming the great seducer [*Verführer*]."*

The perversion of leadership began almost at once, while a screen of "state rectitude" seemed to conceal the Nazis' many illegal acts. To boot, Hitler and his chieftains were cunning, ruthless improvisers: they instantly exploited the Reichstag fire on February 27 (which, contrary to speculation at the time, they probably did not themselves set) to have President Hindenburg sign emergency decrees that suspended the basic civil rights guaranteed by the Weimar Constitution (neither the constitution nor these decrees were ever abrogated). Thus, thirty days into his reign Hitler could "legally" crush his political enemies and place them in "protective custody" (the Nazis' euphemistic term for imprisonment and worse); intimidate the general public; and organize violent acts on city streets and in meetings,

---

Dietrich Bonhoeffer Works, Vol. 8, p. 247. The broadcast was truncated, so Bonhoeffer's ending was cut off before that very sentence. He drafted a round-robin letter to many pastors explaining that the broadcast's abrupt ending had come "at a most inappropriate place, most likely to give rise to false interpretations," but the simple reason for it was that he had run over his allotted time, so the sentence that had meant the most to him was not heard. Overheated interpretations of this truncation nonetheless abound. And the broadcast was not, as some writers wrongly assume, his first act of resistance. See *Dietrich Bonhoeffer Werke*, Vol. 12, p. 47.

with houses and offices searched, mail intercepted, phones tapped, and the press intermittently muzzled.

In this transformed, ominous climate, Germans voted on March 5 in their last "free" election. (The Nazis obtained just under 44 percent of the vote, only barely mustering a majority with their conservative allies.) A week later, in a great pageant at the Hohenzollerns' historic Garrison Church in Potsdam, Hindenburg and Hitler appeared together, each paying tribute to what the other stood for: it was the apparent union of old conservatives with a young, *völkische* desire for Germany's national rebirth. But woe to nonbelievers: soon thousands of people were arrested, and when the press reported on the opening of the new Dachau concentration camp near Munich for political prisoners (there were soon many other camps, too), the news was accompanied by official photographs of prominent Weimar politicians in prison garb, being "reeducated."

Bonhoeffer most probably voted for the Catholic Center Party as he had already done in July 1932, saying then to Franz Hildebrandt, "The only thing that matters now is to keep the Nazis from gaining power."* But within just a few weeks the Center Party voted with the National Socialists so that Hitler had the two-thirds majority in the Reichstag he needed to pass the Enabling Act, which gave his much-vaunted coalition government—constitutionally!—four years of virtually unlimited power. (The only deputies opposing the Enabling Act were the Social Democrats—in their bravest moment. Communists were banned from participating.) The Nazis swiftly subordinated all public activity to their will; this infamous *Gleichschaltung*

---

*Roggelin, *Franz Hildebrandt*, p. 44. Roggelin notes that Bethge, in his biography of Bonhoeffer, wrongly ascribes this exchange to the March 1933 election, thus missing Bonhoeffer's shrewd political foresight.

had an astounding, rapid success, thanks to the public's widespread support or subservience, and its fears of the regime's terror.

On April 7 the regime promulgated its cynically named Law for the Restoration of the Professional Civil Service, with its "Aryan clause" proscribing all "non-Aryans" from holding any civil service position—a category that included professors, judges, and some doctors.* Within weeks, judges and attorneys of Jewish descent were "retired" from their posts. The universities were purged, the ousted victims often assaulted and dishonored—and there were hardly any protests anywhere. The University of Frankfurt am Main was so hard hit by the racial and political dismissals that there was talk about closing it down entirely. Yet in this transformed landscape some scholars fared well. Carl Schmitt offers the best example: in July he moved to the law faculty at the University of Berlin and began his notorious rise to become the Nazis' top legal expert—a position he lost in 1936, however.[26] Already in 1933, along with another ardently Nazi lawyer, Roland Freisler, Schmitt urged eliminating the very word *Rechtsstaat* from German discourse; he called it "a pathbreaker

---

*In one realm, the Nazis were more successful than they could have dreamed they might be: the sudden ubiquity, after this law, of the habit of labeling people by racial "identity." The tens of thousands of German Jews who since the early nineteenth century had taken the step of converting to Christianity and who had simply been "Germans" became again, and still are—in the view of many friends, all enemies, and most historians—"Jews," from Heinrich Heine to Felix Mendelssohn to Fritz Haber. This was partly a matter of convenience: after the defeat of the Nazis, "non-Aryan" became an impossible category, and it seemed easier to draw the line between "Christians" and "Jews." A minority among baptized German Jews, Gert Leibholz included, felt a deepening of their Christian consciousness; among others the sense of Jewish identity became strong; and in many more instances the individual slipped into secular indifference. But that the great Germans of the past who had been born to converted Jewish families were again "Jews" was a source of confusion for their descendants and the unknowing general public.

for liberal democracy, Jewry, and Marxism." As we shall see, the effort to maintain the *Rechtsstaat*, or at least shreds of it, occupied Hans von Dohnanyi in particular.

Dietrich quickly wrote letters on behalf of some "non-Aryan" professors and affirmed his support for Karl Barth (at Göttingen) and Paul Tillich (at Frankfurt), theologians who for other reasons were in danger of losing their university positions.* But aside from courageous letters expressive of his personal decency, what forms did Bonhoeffer's opposition to Hitler take? That the German Evangelical Church would be a principal target for Hitler had been obvious from the start, and from the start Bonhoeffer threw himself into the work of countering Nazi actions regarding it. Virtually everything he did to maintain his ecumenical contacts, his theological study, and his pastoral work set him against the Nazifying church authorities.

In truth many, perhaps most, Protestant bishops and pastors were supporters of the regime. Bonhoeffer witnessed compliant clerics timorously equivocating on the Nazis' revision of church doctrine, welcoming Hitler's plan to transform the churches' federation into a single conformist Reich Church, and eagerly implementing Nazi orders about church administration at every level. All too many pastors converted their old-fashioned anti-Weimar conservatism into support for Nazi appeals for "national regeneration and sacrifice," along with exhortations to young people who might be fed up with what

---

*In 1933, right after storm troopers marched into the University of Frankfurt, the socialist Tillich, chair of the philosophy department, went to the Education Ministry to inquire about his status and got into an argument there about the Jewish sources of Christianity, on which he insisted; he was fired. Tillich left Germany—but reluctantly, for he was worried about his many Jewish colleagues and friends. When Barth wrote to the same ministry to ask the same question, he indicated that he intended to remain a member of the Social Democratic Party, which doomed him; in 1935 he was dismissed from the Bonn faculty when he refused to swear the required oath of loyalty to Hitler, and left Germany for his native Switzerland.

was called "Weimar liberalism." In common right-wing parlance, liberalism had come to mean sanctimonious indecisiveness; the historic link between liberalism and freedom was forgotten.

Publicly and energetically Bonhoeffer and a few other conscientious pastors tried to rally their colleagues to challenge the imposition of the Aryan clause on the German Evangelical Church and to rebuff the Nazi pastors' efforts to impose their anti-Semitic standards on them all. But this was not easy; some of the "German Christians" had for years been proud to proclaim themselves the "SA of Christ," and they were ruthless. (An oft-repeated parable of 1934 has a Breslau pastor open the Sunday service by asking all non-Aryans to leave the church; after repeating the order for the third time, the figure on the Cross disappears.)

In 1932, Dietrich had joined a pastors' study group in Berlin where he had enjoyed vigorous discussions with other clerics—on the correct or incorrect grounds for pacifism, for example—but he had found his colleagues weak in their theology, and his mind kept drifting off to his hopes for another trip somewhere, maybe India, which had long fascinated him (an old longing to learn about Gandhi and nonviolent resistance, an old wish to be "elsewhere"). The group became livelier as the political situation deteriorated, however; by 1933 some in the group thought they should discuss the *Judenfrage*—the Jewish question—by which they meant the question of what should be done about church members from once-Jewish families that might well have been baptized Christians for generations. Also, what were they supposed to do with the regime's order that fellow clergy in this category should be defrocked? Others didn't want to deal with the second issue, which after all affected only a handful of men, but Bonhoeffer thought they should and must. It was an opportunity to declare—or, to use the church term, confess—the fundamental tenets of their Christian faith.

At the very beginning of this Nazi war to gain control of the Evangelical Church—the *Kirchenkampf*—Bonhoeffer wrote an essay entitled "The Church and the Jewish Question." Some scholars focus on what they regard as anti-Semitic in this essay, given the passages in it citing Luther's well-known view that Jewish suffering was punishment for the Crucifixion (a doctrine to which Roman Catholics also adhered) and suggesting that the best outcome would be for Jews to convert to Christianity, the religion that, for Luther as for Catholics, supersedes Judaism. But there was far more to Bonhoeffer's essay than that.

The twenty-seven-year-old author, good Lutheran that he was, conceded at the start that the church had no right to judge state actions—"It has neither to praise nor to censure the laws of the state"— but he insisted that it could and should ask whether a state action (for example vis-à-vis Jews) "can be justified as...legitimate." This was already farther than many of his seniors wanted to go. Secondly, he argued, the church had an "unconditional obligation toward the victims of any ordering of society, even if they do not belong to the Christian community," and in any case a "baptized Jew is a member of our church." His insistence here on what ethicists call "the responsibility to protect" is an early demonstration of a crucial element in Bonhoeffer's theology. Thirdly—here was the point that has been most cited—the church must "not only bind up the wounds of those who have fallen beneath the wheel" of the state "but at times halt the wheel itself." This largely defiant, albeit slightly accommodating, essay could be still be published in June 1933.[27] (In 1967, Barth admitted that he had not realized at the time that Bonhoeffer "was the first and almost only pastor to grasp and deal with the centrality of the *Judenfrage*. For a long time I have felt my own guilt that in the *Kirchenkampf* I didn't, at least not publicly, acknowledge the centrality of the issue."[28])

The fluctuating, time-consuming battle to keep the churches Christian, as Bonhoeffer saw it, seemed never-ending. He and the very few other anti-Nazi ministers despaired of prevailing. "The Jewish question," he told a Swiss friend in April, had made "even the most intelligent people [lose] their heads and their Bibles," and these political struggles obscured the centrality of pastoral work, "which is alone what matters in the church. I often long terribly for a quiet pastorate," he wrote.[29] But he kept at it, as did Hildebrandt.

Both of these young men became known to another dissenter, and an important one: Martin Niemöller, a fearless pastor of celebrated valor (he had been a U-boat captain in the Great War), changing political allegiances (he had voted for the National Socialists and then came to regret it), and divergent views (he was an anti-Semite *and* an anti-Nazi, a not unusual combination), who presided over an important church in the Berlin suburb of Dahlem. At a low point in mid-1933 the three men briefly thought that perhaps they must leave the Evangelical Church, abandon it to its German Christian destroyers. But this was theologically and politically unacceptable. No, the anti-Nazi pastors had to argue that they were the true church and German Christians, along with their fellow travelers, were the godless, pagan betrayers.

Niemöller helped Bonhoeffer to formulate one of several new confessions of faith for the dissenters: the Bethel Confession of September 1933, which to Bonhoeffer's exasperation got badly watered down, especially when some pastors deleted its rejection of the Aryan clause. Bonhoeffer, Hildebrandt, and others agreed that a "ministry that has become a privilege for Aryans" was not a true Christian church (as Bonhoeffer put it to Barth), and they decided to organize a Pastors' Emergency League for those who wanted to lead "free" churches, as they put it. Within months this was to become the hub of the resistant group known as the Confessing Church, founded in

April–May 1934, which more than two thousand pastors joined. (That was a little more than 10 percent of Germany's total, a fraction roughly balancing the German Christians, with most Protestant leaders hovering in between.) At least the lines were drawn and a valuable reaffirmation of principles was achieved.

It was valuable but insufficient. Bonhoeffer was irritated and disappointed by the pastors' frequent backsliding and their timorous, halting responses to the Nazi operatives in the church administrations. Once again he was torn by uncertainty: Should he perhaps be done with this unpromising mess and accept instead the position offered to him as pastor to a German church in London, where he could work in peace and quiet, and develop his ecumenical work unharassed? He sensed that saving the church in this evil time was going to require even more of true Christians than they had yet volunteered, that these early skirmishes were but provisional engagements. Soon there would be a "transition to an entirely different kind of opposition," he wrote to his Swiss friend Erwin Sutz in early 1934. "And I believe that the whole of Christendom must pray with us that the resistance becomes a 'resistance unto death'... and that people will be found ready to suffer for this purpose."[30]

In October 1933 Bonhoeffer said goodbye to his students in Berlin and went off to London for eighteen months. But he kept himself informed of Germany's shocking march to a totalitarian order—with people dismissed from their posts, others disappearing into concentration camps, books burned in front of ancient universities, the press muzzled, and the churches torn this way and that. It is often forgotten how much, in those first Nazi months, the German public was willing to put up with—whether out of acceptance, perhaps with regret about the "excesses," or out of fear. The Bonhoeffers were certainly alive to the dangers of the terroristic regime the Nazis were imposing so swiftly.

Bonhoeffer's time in London was hardly a respite from hard work and tension. There were the rigors of weekly preaching at his church; he also helped some newly arrived German émigrés, of which there were now many, to find homes and jobs; and, inevitably, he led efforts to persuade the German congregations in England to join the Confessing Church. Also, he made new friends among English, Scandinavian, and Swiss clerics who were alarmed about the life-and-death struggle going on in the German church and ready to intervene if they could on behalf of those resisting the Nazis. He found a special ally in George Bell, the bishop of Chichester and chairman of the ecumenists' Council on Life and Work. Bell liked him. Recommending Bonhoeffer to another cleric, Bell wrote, "He is under 30, unmarried, and speaks English perfectly. He is extraordinarily critical of the present rulers of the German church."[31]

Most important was the time Bonhoeffer spent on intense study of the Sermon on the Mount and on what "discipleship" truly entailed. This focus on the Sermon on the Mount sometimes exasperated his Confessing Church colleagues, but he knew what he was doing: the spiritual practice of meditating on this impossible, sublime text greatly strengthened and deepened him. He rightly believed that it was being forgotten or ignored in the conventions of modern Christian practice—isn't it still?—and it remained at the core of his religious study for the rest of his short life, at the core of his spiritual being.

Dietrich was not the only Bonhoeffer whose world was profoundly altered by the Nazis. Dr. Bonhoeffer confronted the ministry (and his Nazified colleagues) on many issues, most often those concerning the fate of "non-Aryan" colleagues, whom he helped as much as he could. And the oldest son, Karl-Friedrich, by 1930 a professor of physical chemistry in Frankfurt, was aghast to learn in 1933 that his mentor, the Nobel laureate chemist Fritz Haber, had resigned from the directorship of his Kaiser Wilhelm Institute in Berlin, since to stay on (which, as a veteran of the Great War, he could have done, though he was a converted Jew) he would have been required to dismiss his Jewish colleagues, which he would not do. When Haber died in exile less than a year later and the physicist Max Planck (Harnack's successor as president of the Kaiser Wilhelm Society) arranged a memorial for him in Berlin despite the Nazis' wish to extinguish his memory, Karl-Friedrich wrote a warm tribute to Haber, but the Nazis forbade civil servants from attending the service, so the celebrated chemist Otto Hahn, who had resigned from Berlin University, read it on his behalf.

Each of the lawyers in the family—Klaus Bonhoeffer and the three brothers-in-law Rüdiger Schleicher, Hans von Dohnanyi, and Gert Leibholz, along with the almost-family Justus Delbrück—faced, in different ways, the Nazis' assaults on the very essence of the law, not to mention the unremitting Nazi attacks on Jewish lawyers and lawyers deemed politically "unreliable." Despite the growing risks, they engaged in oppositional, then resistant acts; eventually this resistance work took over their lives.

Dohnanyi's outstanding career during the Weimar years had started right after his law studies, when he was appointed to the team preparing the Foreign Ministry's collection of documents on Germany's pre-1914 foreign policy; from there he was appointed the assistant to Albrecht Mendelssohn-Bartholdy,* head of a newly founded Institute of Foreign Affairs in Hamburg, in 1924. The four ensuing years in Hamburg were immensely busy and successful. In addition to his work at the institute, Dohnanyi pursued further legal studies at the university and earned his doctorate. He wrote, he lectured, and

---

*The historian Felix Gilbert, a descendant of the celebrated Mendelssohn-Bartholdy family, was a close friend of both Dohnanyi and Dietrich Bonhoeffer, and he succeeded Dohnanyi in the Foreign Ministry job.

he became known as an energetic, ambitious man of exceptional intellect and integrity. He expressed his democratic convictions and his deeply felt loyalty to the Republic—a rare attitude, particularly among young, upwardly mobile legal scholars. Briefly he also served in Hamburg's civil administration.

It was in Hamburg that Christine, a budding botanist, reluctantly gave up her science to assume the traditional wifely, motherly role in their growing family. In 1929 they returned to Berlin when Hans entered the Ministry of Justice working for State Secretary Curt Jöel (like Mendelssohn-Bartholdy a converted Jew). With his passionate interest in Weimar politics and his unconditional, patriotic support of the Republic, Hans was, like Rüdiger Schleicher, more fervent and outspoken in his democratic convictions than other family members. Converted Jews were among his closest friends and admired superiors—an additional reason for him to find Nazi anti-Semitism repellent.

In June 1933, Dohnanyi became the chief assistant to Franz Gürtner, a former Bavarian minister of justice. In 1932 Gürtner had willingly become Reich minister of justice under Chancellor Franz von Papen and then under Kurt von Schleicher—he favored their authoritarian plans; like them he had no use for the Weimar Republic or for democratizing reforms of any sort. But as Hitler's state developed its totalitarian form, Gürtner, a genuine conservative, found himself fighting—and losing—battles to retain the last vestiges of a legal order. He had to participate (as did, occasionally, his aide Dohnanyi) in interministerial deliberations on a Nazified penal code, for example; nothing came of that particular effort, but Gürtner was coming to understand the criminality of the regime. Dohnanyi went with Gürtner to an appointment with Hitler that first summer at his new retreat at Obersalzberg. On his return, Christine recalled, he told her, "The man is mad."

Gürtner stuck to his post, though, "to prevent worse from happening." A genuine servant of the law, he had to facilitate its degradation into violence.[32] And Hans knew that, as Marikje Smid wrote, he too "had become against his will a part of the National Socialist system." At one point Gürtner said to Christine, "National Socialism is a feverish disease of the German people. And as long as the fever lasts, a doctor cannot leave the patient's bed, even when he thinks there is nothing more he can do." Obviously there are many ways to read this sentence, but that it depicts a sharp inner conflict should be acknowledged.[33]

Hitler had kept Gürtner on so as to reassure people that the "law" remained in non-Nazi hands. But the Gestapo and Heinrich Himmler's SS (Schutzstaffel), aiming at virtually full autonomy and unlimited power, kept the Justice Ministry under surveillance.

Still, as Gürtner's confidant, Dohnanyi usually knew ahead of time about new laws being planned by the Nazis, and he passed on useful, important information to his brother-in-law; Dietrich in turn kept him abreast of the ecclesiastical conflicts. And he also advised colleagues and friends who had become victims of Nazi rule. To Christine, he called this work, often conducted in his office, "my *Privatpraxis*," a term borrowed from the medical profession.[34]

Even more remarkably, with cool-headed efficiency and rising outrage Dohnanyi began to keep a chronological record, along with supporting evidence and an index, of the regime's illegal acts. These documents were meant to facilitate the prosecution of Nazi criminals after the end of the regime. He began this in October 1934, after the Prussian and Reich ministries of justice were merged and Gürtner appointed him as the chief of his ministerial office. He kept track of the details of particular measures taken against clergy and Jews, and of the many instances when the party, the Gestapo, the SA, and the SS violated legal norms—from arbitrary detentions and torture to currency swindles and other financial crimes committed by local Nazi chieftains; eventually the file (in postwar years it came to be called the "Chronicle of Shame") included documentation on the persecution of

Jews, details and evidence about Nazi atrocities in Poland in 1939 and in the east after 1941. Gürtner knew about this record-keeping and apparently approved of it. (And he allowed Dohnanyi to keep the documents even when he left the Ministry of Justice.) The records were stored in an army safe, Dohnanyi having been assured of its inviolability, at the military base in Zossen, some twenty miles from Berlin.

Like all civil servants, Dohnanyi had to submit proof of unblemished Aryan descent—but he could not. The files yielded incriminating information that his maternal grandfather was Jewish. In 1936, in a routine meeting with Hitler, Gürtner told him there were some difficulties with his indispensable personal deputy, but Hitler declared, "Dohnanyi should not suffer any disadvantage because of his racial origins [*Abstammung*]."[35] Still, it wasn't until March 1940 that Dohnanyi received official confirmation of his and his sister's racial "purity." The fervent Nazi Roland Freisler, a fellow lawyer in the Justice Ministry and already a political and personal enemy of Dohnanyi's, indirectly called for a ministerial inquiry, which ended with a report sent to Hitler's deputy labeling Dohnanyi as "half German, quarter Hungarian, and quarter Jew."

When Dietrich was back in Berlin for a while in 1934, the church crisis reached another boiling point when the Confessing Church, in its inaugural Barmen Declaration (much of it drafted by Barth and welcomed by ecumenical churchmen in England, the United States, and Scandinavia), insisted that it was "the lawful Evangelical Church in Germany" and repudiated the German Christians' "false teaching and false doctrine." It is theologically a quite conventional Protestant statement of the "evangelical truths" concerning the primacy of God's revelation in the incarnate Word. Still, the passionate debate among the Lutherans over whether and how to acknowledge the "errors of the 'German Christians' and of the present Reich Church Administration, which are ravaging the Church and at the same time also shattering the unity of the German Evangelical Church," as the declaration put it, was, one historian has written, of an intensity "unparalleled in German Protestantism since the Reformation."[36]

The Nazi offensive against the Evangelical Church ran concurrently with Hitler's efforts to reach a concordat with the Vatican, whose negotiations were led by Cardinal Secretary of State Eugenio Pacelli (the future Pius XII), considered an expert on Germany after his twelve years as papal nuncio in Munich and then Berlin. Hitler had been angered by the German Catholic bishops' early denunciation of what they, too, had called the Nazis' "false doctrines," and wanted moral recognition from the papacy. For his part Pacelli, single-mindedly focused on achieving concordats with various states, especially wanted to assure the rights, privileges, and standing of the German Catholic hierarchy vis-à-vis Germany's new government. The final agreement provided both; it also virtually eliminated the raison d'être of the Center Party, which, three days before the concordat was signed on July 20, dissolved itself, as some other parties had already done; for Hitler this was one less obstacle to the creation of a one-party state. He no more intended to adhere to the concordat's provisions than he adhered to any other commitment.

Meanwhile conservative apprehensions, some of them voiced, about ever more radical Nazi moves pushed Hitler into action. Tensions were also increasing between the SA, now with more than a million members, and the peacetime army, which the Versailles Treaty had specified as a volunteer force of no more than 100,000 (recruits were limited to men committed to serving for twelve years). Rivalries and ugly personal antagonisms reached a lethal climax on June 30, 1934, the Night of the Long Knives, when Hitler ordered the murders, by roving death squads of SS men and Gestapo agents, of both Ernst Röhm, the leader of the SA and Hitler's longtime intimate, and two army generals (and the wife of one of them), as well as dozens of public figures (among them leading lay Catholics) whom he wanted out of the way. Dr. Bonhoeffer had rightly noticed Hitler's enthusiasm for political murder. Justice Minister Gürtner paid a price for continuing in office: he had to sign into law a statute that retroactively gave legal sanction to these murderous acts. Hitler boasted of having purged the nation of dangerous elements, the cabinet and President Hindenburg publicly endorsed what had happened, and the regime emerged stronger from the crisis; the SS proved to be the true victor.

Many Germans cheered Hitler for having taken "decisive" action to secure the realm on June 30, for having achieved the concordat with Rome, and, after Hindenburg's death on August 2, for consolidating the two highest offices in the land in his singular new role as "Führer and Reich chancellor of the German people." And the army readily swore an oath of fealty to him despite his unprecedented murder of two of its generals; within a year it was Hitler's army, no longer the Reichswehr but now the Wehrmacht, and on his orders it was disregarding ever more brazenly the limitations imposed by the Versailles Treaty. Dietrich understood the gravity of these developments; writing to Niebuhr in July, he told him that in his circles they were beginning to realize that a *"Kulturkampf* situation" had been reached; he had been surprised that no Evangelical pastor had been among those shot on June 30. (He also appealed to Niebuhr for help for two political refugees.[37])

In London on July 8 Dietrich preached a fiery sermon that was in sharp contrast to the enthusiastic reassurances most Germans were hearing from the pulpit about the bloodbath in the Reich. His text was the famous "repent or perish" passage in the Gospel of Saint Luke,*

---

*"There were present at that season some that told him of Galileans whose blood Pilate had mingled with their sacrifices. And Jesus answering said unto them, Suppose ye that these Galileans were sinners above all the Galileans because they suffered such things? I tell you, Nay: but, except ye repent, ye shall all likewise perish" (Luke 13:1–3).

and while he made it very clear that he considered it inappropriate, even dangerous, to bring current events into a church service, his central pastoral point was that turning one's back on worldly crises, or trying to forget them, or dissociating oneself from them was as foolish as exulting in them. The meaning of Jesus's instruction is quite different: one must accept that it is not for us to judge or condemn or praise; rather, we must recognize the sins in our own hearts, repent, "and realize that no human being is ever right in the end." Accepting this spiritual truth is difficult, and the repentant sinner's situation is dangerous, for "we are no longer spectators, observers, judges...now we ourselves are the ones addressed, we are the ones affected. God is speaking to us. It is meant for us....Lord, lead your people to repent and begin with us."[38]

Whether in London or Berlin, Dietrich spent most of that summer preparing for, and then working at, a conference of the Ecumenical Council (the Faith and Order group) on the Danish island of Fanö in August, where the most urgent topic was whether this international body should recognize the Confessing Church or the German Christians as speaking for Protestant Germany. He wrote ahead of time to warn the Danish bishop in charge that Dietrich's anti-Nazi brethren might be timorous: "I am more worried about many of our own people than about the German Christians....[They act as they do] not so much because of anxiety as because of a wrongly understood sense of honor....If only, honorable Bishop, you could succeed in breaking this ice, in gaining the trust of these men and opening them up!" He felt strongly that the delegates must acknowledge that "the time is very near when we shall have to decide between National Socialism and Christianity."[39]

Dietrich made an unforgettable impression on the international crowd of theology students when he preached in his compelling manner on a text he loved, Psalm 85: "I will hear what God the Lord will speak: for he will speak peace unto his people, and to his saints: but let them not turn again to folly. Surely his salvation is nigh them that fear him; that glory may dwell in our land." The fame of this homily, Bonhoeffer's "peace sermon," long outlasted the Third Reich. But for the Nazis, who were preaching manly bellicosity, peace was the last concern.

With autumn came a return to Berlin. Bonhoeffer's intention now was to teach pastors-to-be, work he could combine with studying and writing. But this was not easily arranged: he needed to have his educational work accorded legitimate authority, and Nazi-compliant church officials refused to sanction Confessing Church seminaries. Equally, Bonhoeffer refused to make any concessions to the Reich Christians. Even some of his closest allies sometimes thought that his absolute opposition to any compromise with the Reich Church was stubbornly intransigent. By 1936 the Gestapo forbade him to give lectures at the University of Berlin, but by then he had arranged to teach divinity students and mentor ordinands at Finkenwalde, a remote country estate in Pomerania where the Church of the Old Prussian Union had founded a quasi-legitimate "preachers' seminary," one of four to replace those that Reich Church officials had closed. Beginning in April 1935 Finkenwalde, where Eberhard Bethge was among the first students, became the center of Dietrich's professional life.

In a letter of January 1935 to his brother Karl-Friedrich (now living and working in Leipzig), Dietrich wrote that although he had started off thinking of theological studies as a fairly academic matter, "now it has turned into something else entirely. But I do believe that at last I am on the right track, for the first time in my life."[40] His joyous strength as a teacher-pastor matured and deepened over the three Finkenwalde years, as if increase of appetite grew by what it fed on.

And this spiritual power is evident in everything he wrote later, notably in his most famous book, *The Cost of Discipleship*, the core of which is an exegesis of the Sermon on the Mount. His exasperation with the tedious, hair-splitting maneuvers among German clergy over how, when, and whether to disobey Nazi strictures is clear in his letter to Karl-Friedrich:

> I believe I know that inwardly I shall be really clear and honest
> only when I have begun to take the Sermon on the Mount seriously. That is the only source of strength that can blow all this
> stuff and nonsense sky-high, with only a few charred pieces of
> the fireworks remaining. The restoration of the church will
> [only] come from . . . a life of uncompromising adherence to the
> Sermon on the Mount in imitation of Christ.[41]

After Hitler defiantly announced the introduction of universal military conscription in 1935, his clearest violation yet of the Versailles Treaty, Dietrich had to confront his haunting dread of being drafted—first as a remote possibility and then as an inescapable certainty. He felt a powerful prohibition against donning a military uniform and taking the nefarious oath to the Führer: that was a lie he could not live with. And since the Nazis usually punished "conscientious objectors" with death sentences, he did not think he could consider this option. With his inner revulsion against military service under Hitler, perhaps the fate of his brother Walter drifted through his mind; the biographies do not mention this, but the passionate urgency with which Dietrich worried about his conscription suggests very deep emotions. And always he thought of his family, which fully supported him and remained steadfast in many modes of opposition to the regime.

By then, some in the family were already engaged in the most audacious form of opposition: working in public office as a cover for
subversive activity against the state. Hans von Dohnanyi was shoul-
dering this dual burden, his vulnerability on account of his racial
"stigma" notwithstanding, and so was Rüdiger Schleicher, in the legal
department of Hermann Göring's Air Ministry. (Despite his deepest
misgivings, he joined the Nazi Party in order to keep his position—
and its subversive possibilities.*) There was also Klaus Bonhoeffer,
by 1935 a chief lawyer for Lufthansa, a position that permitted him
to take trips abroad that he then could use for clandestine resistance
purposes, and Klaus's brother-in-law Justus Delbrück, who was soon
to join the active resistance.

All these men and their families had by now become adepts of
secretive communication—writing with ciphers, speaking on the
telephone in agreed-upon codes, hiding messages—daily practices of
camouflage and dissimulation that anti-Nazis had to adopt if they
wished to get on with life. Hans became well practiced in using ironic
exaggeration to convey his impressions of what was going on. Soon,
some among them had to take it further: they had to plan how they
would keep in touch were they to be arrested and jailed. The Bonhoeffers decided how they would use books delivered to prisoners as
message devices, putting tiny dots under letters spread out over many
pages that together spelled out instructions, warnings, news, or loving notes of support; they learned how to write in minuscule script on
tiny bits of paper or cardboard that could be buried at the bottom of

---

*"On the evening of the last possible day before the deadline for registration in the party in
May 1933, my father paced back and forth with me in front of the door to the party office
until the office closed and he had to knock in order to be able to declare his entry into
the party." Hans-Walter Schleicher, in Bethge and Bethge, *Last Letters of Resistance*,
p. 10.

a jar of food or hidden in a bunch of flowers*; they trained themselves to speak to each other in the presence of police or other officers without giving anything away. Among people who to the core of their being valued honesty and truth, these techniques, which only the most urgent crisis permitted, aroused a sometimes comic spirit and at other times moral repugnance.

Dietrich Bonhoeffer's work at Finkenwalde was in one respect sharply focused, though in some lights it might seem shapeless. Days, weeks, months were spent in quasi-monastic, shabby settings; he and his students committed themselves to long days of study, prayer, services (generously laced with music), meditation on assigned biblical texts (a controversial practice of which some disapproved), and classes on pastoral and homiletic subjects. This pastoral-educational work was punctuated by frequent phone calls to his parents in Berlin (mostly to his mother) and occasional trips; he also kept up an impressively large correspondence with colleagues, fellow pastors, Finkenwalde alumni, and friends.

In 1937 the regime came down hard on the Confessing Church: over the summer the Gestapo arrested or rearrested more than eight hundred of its pastors. Thousands of church members were thus deprived of spiritual guidance. Dohnanyi met with Niemöller and did what he could to help him and other pastors.[42] The regime was now forbidding all intercessory prayers in Confessing Church services for those who were absent, or suffering, or grieving, and also outlawed the taking up of collections, which after all were a main source of funds for each parish's pastoral work; further restrictive regulations

---

*In 2012, an impressive exhibition of "Secrets: Forbidden Messages" from around the world was mounted by the Deutsche Schillergesellschaft in Marbach. It included an extraordinary smuggled letter of 1945 from the imprisoned Dohnanyi to his wife. See below, pp. 123–124.

were handed down by the Ministry of Church Affairs (working in cooperation with the Interior Ministry). And on Himmler's express orders Finkenwalde was closed down.

On July 1 Bonhoeffer, along with Hildebrandt and Bethge, had gone to Niemöller's parsonage to confer with him about the alarming news of these arrests and arrived only moments after Gestapo agents had taken Niemöller away.* Being kept there under house arrest for seven hours as the agents pawed through the pastor's papers and belongings was unpleasant for all three, but worst for Hildebrandt, who knew what the next steps for him would be. In 1934, he had resigned from his post in Berlin when the churches had accepted the Aryan clause, knowing his position was at risk because his mother was Jewish; he had briefly joined Dietrich in London and then had returned to Germany at Niemöller's request to help in building up the Pastors' Emergency League. Now the Gestapo had him in its sights; it arrested him within a few weeks. Friends, including the Bonhoeffers, made discreet, high-level efforts to gain his release after a month; once freed, Hildebrandt quickly fled to London and a life in exile. Germany had lost an exemplary pastor and Bonhoeffer an exuberant colleague whose amity and intellectual companionship he had enjoyed for years.

---

*Niemöller was jailed for eight months, released, and then, on the very same day, the Gestapo rearrested him and sent him first to the concentration camp in Sachsenhausen, then to Dachau, where he was incarcerated until May 1945. At the outbreak of war in 1939, he volunteered for active military duty and was turned down; many of his friends and supporters abroad regretted this puzzling gesture.

III

HITLER'S DEFIANCE AND deception of the West was continuing apace. In March 1936 he had announced, in a dramatic speech to the Nazified Reichstag, that at that very moment German troops were re-entering the Rhineland, which had been demilitarized under the Versailles Treaty. This breach of the established order had been followed instantly by pious plans for European peace. But Hitler divulged his real intentions in a confidential talk with his six principal military chiefs on November 5, 1937, in which he outlined his plans for war and a New Order in Europe.

When Hans von Dohnanyi heard about this, he instantly understood its importance and conferred at once with like-minded opponents of the regime. More than a few Wehrmacht officers were shocked by the irresponsibility of Hitler's plans. How could this march to war be stopped? Was there any other option but the removal of Hitler? They could not see one. And if that was the only solution, by what means would it be achieved? Obviously their conversations required discretion and secrecy in carefully camouflaged settings, for there was surveillance everywhere, safety nowhere.

Hitler was also manipulating a new crisis within the military leadership, for both his minister of war, Field Marshal Werner von

Blomberg, and his army commander in chief, General Werner von Fritsch, were opposed to his war plans. These officers would have to be purged, and Hitler dealt with them by exploiting a sordid calamity in the first case and falsifying records in the second. The widowed Blomberg had impulsively decided to marry a rather common woman thirty-five years his junior and Hitler had happily agreed to be a witness at the wedding (Göring was best man) in early January 1938— only to learn soon after that the new wife was very common indeed: in 1932 she had posed for pornographic pictures taken by a Jew with whom she was then living and had been arrested; in 1933 the police had registered her as a prostitute. So Blomberg had to go. And the Gestapo blackmailed his likely successor, the very popular, well-regarded General Fritsch, on a trumped-up charge about an alleged homosexual relationship some years earlier. He too had to go.

Dohnanyi was sickened by the baseness of these illegal maneuvers, disgusted by Fritsch's removal, and troubled by the new army structure Hitler invented, with a Supreme High Command of the Armed Forces under Field Marshal Wilhelm Keitel, a spineless officer who was totally subservient to the Führer and consumed by his own vanity. Dohnanyi continued his contacts with some of the disaffected officers.

In conjunction with his recasting of the Wehrmacht command, Hitler rid his government of its remaining old "conservatives" and replaced them with, in most instances, incompetent party minions. The most fateful change was the dismissal of Foreign Minister Konstantin von Neurath and the appointment in his place of the vain, supine Joachim von Ribbentrop, then Germany's ineffectual ambassador to Great Britain. This left State Secretary Ernst von Weizsäcker —hesitant about Germany going to war, hesitant about any further radicalization of foreign policy—in a very isolated position in the fully Nazified Foreign Ministry. He knew of the ever-widening atrocities being perpetrated against Jews, but to some extent he also abetted Nazi policies. Hjalmar Schacht, faithful custodian of currency stability as minister of finance and president of the Reichsbank, was also dismissed. Both Weizsäcker and Schacht had shreds of decency left, and they had sometimes tried to help endangered individuals. Weizsäcker, whom some of the conspirators were occasionally in touch with and who knew of their aims and activities, neither joined nor betrayed them. (His career remains a deeply contested subject in the history of Germany.[43]) These changes signaled the further radicalization of the Nazi regime; there were few brakes left. Dohnanyi and the other plotters recognized how isolated and vulnerable they were.

Hitler, that ex-corporal from the Great War, a man both megalomaniacal and paranoid, had always distrusted the Reichswehr generals. He also believed that he had already proved to them and the world his own superior, indeed infallible judgment in his daring and dramatic moves. And he had altered Europe's military balance in Germany's favor. Now, in the spring of 1938, he defied all obstacles and managed the *Anschluss* with Austria.

In addition to his international successes, Hitler could boast of a booming economy at home. Unemployment had been all but eliminated, somehow Germany had carried out a huge rearmament program without incurring inflation, and its network of new autobahns was hailed as the visible sign of modernization (obscuring its strategic utility). Germany's fabled Zeppelins flew over the Atlantic where German submarines were once again prowling (a bilateral treaty with England officially allowed this). Many people abroad, especially conservatives, admired these rapidly consolidated achievements. Not for the last time were they impressed, perhaps enviously impressed, by such material triumphs, even when accompanied by domestic repression. Within Germany, however, the atmosphere had become grim. Normality and sudden dread coexisted.

The tempo of Hitler's aggressions was accelerating. Having brought Austria into the Reich, next he was determined to "bring home" the almost three million ethnic Germans in the Sudetenland, a territory of Czechoslovakia adjoining both Germany and Austria. This would surely destroy Czechoslovakia, which was Central Europe's only remaining democracy—and a militarily strong one.

The army officers who knew of Hitler's plans and wanted to stop him from implementing them realized that if they were going to mount a putsch against him they would have to do so very soon, before he initiated hostilities against Czechoslovakia. Dohnanyi became close to these conspirators, notably to General Ludwig Beck, chief of the general staff, and to a remarkable officer named Hans Oster, a pastor's son who since 1933 had been in military intelligence, the Abwehr, where he was now the deputy to its chief, Admiral Wilhelm Canaris, another conspirator. Oster had an almost visceral loathing of Hitler, whom he called "the pig," but his resistance work, like that of the others, was animated by high political and moral principles.

The plotters were looking for more recruits for their loosely organized network, and they were expanding their scope: some worked on plans for the putsch and its immediate aftermath, others thought about the moral and political order that in the long term should follow Nazi nihilism. They also wanted to obtain from Neville Chamberlain's government some indication that they could count on British support for a generous and respectful treatment of a post-Hitler German government: no second Versailles! Some of the more conservative among them even hoped that this new Germany might retain its most recent territorial gains.

General Beck was the essential figure in any effort to overthrow Hitler, for only high Wehrmacht officers had proximity to him and the potential power to depose him. Beck, a man of learning with a deep sense of responsibility, was a true patriot, a critical lover of his country, and he had once been an early sympathizer with National Socialist aims to restore German strength. But in 1938 he openly argued against Hitler's scheme to attack Czechoslovakia in order to seize the Sudetenland and at the same time he made covert plans with other officers to remove the Führer from office as soon as possible and to take him prisoner. (In the process Dr. Bonhoeffer would, it was presumed, be ready to examine Hitler and certify him as clinically unstable.*) Beck resigned from the general staff in mid-August when his protestations against Hitler's war policy went for naught (though he consented to Hitler's demand to postpone a public announcement of his resignation), and this, ironically, freed him to devote himself more fully to active work with the men who were going ahead with preparations for a coup in September. But crucial officers were still uncertain, clinging to their infamous oath of loyalty to the Führer to excuse their convenient passivity.

In the end, it was the Western policy of appeasement that put paid to a September putsch. That abject policy—a composite of illusions and genuine eagerness to avoid another war—allowed Hitler to

---

*Dr. Bonhoeffer had to retire the same year. The issue of who would be his successor became predictably, and intensely, controversial. The faculty submitted three names; the ministry wanted the SS member Dr. Max de Crinis. The faculty asked Bonhoeffer for his assessment of one of de Crinis's books: his response was that it was "superficial" (by implication "unscientific"); he didn't even want to keep a copy of it. De Crinis was appointed on November 1, 1938, whereupon many of Bonhoeffer's chief assistants resigned. A competent scholar has judged that all of Dr. Bonhoeffer's efforts to preserve even a degree of scientific autonomy in the Third Reich failed. There continues to be controversy about his position on euthanasia and forced sterilization (see below, pp. 136–137). See Gerrens, *Medizinisches Ethos und theologische Ethik*, chapter 2; and Robert Jütte et al., *Medizin und Nationalsozialismus: Bilanz und Perspektiven der Forschung* (Göttingen: Wallstein, 2011), pp. 214–255.

consolidate his successes and aim for a new one in "solving" the Sudetenland crisis that he had done so much to create. British diplomats busied themselves with efforts to find possible compromises, but these proved pathetically useless and only muddied the waters. Sir Alexander Cadogan, permanent undersecretary in the British Foreign Office, noted on September 21, as frantic negotiations to forestall war continued: "We must go on being cowards up to our limit, but *not beyond*."[44]

Hitler's vile attacks on Czechoslovakia's President Edvard Beneš left no doubt about his aims. And yet a week later, France and Great Britain, at the Munich Conference, agreed that Germany might annex the Sudetenland. This removed the immediate threat of war yet left the rump of Czechoslovakia defenseless and subservient to Germany, which became the dominant power in Europe. But Hitler felt cheated out of a war he had wanted, and he was disappointed. His appetite was unappeasable.

And now he quickened his campaign against Jews in the much-enlarged Gross Deutschland. Dohnanyi, always attentive to the regime's signals of future plans, learned of forthcoming anti-Semitic measures and warned the Leibholzes that they must leave the country at once, which they did—in September 1938, just in time. They emigrated to London, penniless; Gert, shaken, lost his bearings at first, but Sabine, like so many other women in transition to an infinitely difficult new situation, was stalwart. The whole Bonhoeffer family managed to stay in touch with them over the next years.

Franz Gürtner thought that at this point both he and Hans would be safer if Hans left the Justice Ministry, since the Gestapo was shadowing him there so closely. In October 1938 he appointed Hans a judge at the Reichsgericht—the High Court—in Leipzig, where he stayed for a year, the youngest member in its history. But Hans arranged to give weekly lectures in Berlin so that he could see people there and attend the "Thursday meetings" of Beck and Oster in the capital. And he did not forsake the close, confiding relationship that had developed between him and Gürtner; the two of them had been through so much together. He stayed in touch until Gürtner's sudden death in January 1941—a great blow for Hans and his friends.[45]

The Reichsgericht was essentially Nazified by the time Dohnanyi joined it; he was appointed to the second senate, where all but one of his fellow judges were Nazi Party members. Still, some of his colleagues had occasional stirrings of a legal conscience; they reversed a lower-court judgment that had allowed the use of *Beugehaft*, a mild form of coercion used when interrogating prisoners. (It is interesting to reflect that Prussia in 1754 had been the first European state to abolish judicial torture.)

For Hans and his family, the time in Leipzig was a congenial respite: he had time for his family, for music, for new friends, and for quiet reflections with Christine about the future. Life in Leipzig was so much quieter than in Berlin that they considered staying there as a real alternative—but then rejected it. Their resolve to continue at the center of the anti-Hitler resistance in Berlin was clinched with the events of November 9: *Kristallnacht*, with synagogues aflame all over Germany, Jewish properties smashed, and 30,000 Jews arrested.

The Dohnanyis, like Dietrich, were horrified not only by the pogrom but by the craven way that most Germans and their churches responded to this abomination—perhaps uneasily but passively.* In the Bible that Dietrich read for daily meditation and prayer, he marked an exclamation point next to verses from the somber, dramatic Psalm 74, along with the date, "9.xi.38": "They said in their

---

*The European powers hardly behaved better. Only the United States protested this "barbarism" and recalled its ambassador; prominent Americans understood the depth of danger to Western civilization.

hearts, Let us destroy them together: they have burned up all the synagogues of God in the land. We see not our signs: there is no more any prophet: neither is there among us any that knoweth how long. O God, how long shall the adversary reproach? Shall the enemy blaspheme thy name forever?"

The pogrom had been preceded and was followed by new decrees aimed at destroying, by edict, the material existence of German Jews. The *Anschluss*, with its sadistic outbursts by thugs against Jews in Vienna and other cities, had shown one face of anti-Semitism; in Germany the other face was on display, with the hypocritical use of law and even the "spontaneous" violence of *Kristallnacht* minutely organized by the party.

The Wehrmacht conspirators, seeing Hitler's ever-widening aggressions, knew that he was preparing to attack Poland, and knew that this would plunge Germany into a desperately risky war. They resolved once again to do everything they could to stop him. He would have to be removed, and almost certainly, it now seemed, it would have to be by murdering him. *Tyrannenmord* was a literary commonplace among Germans, who knew Schiller's *Wilhelm Tell*, but an actual plan for murder posed serious moral quandaries and huge practical difficulties. All the conspirators worried about the possibility that their countrymen might regard such a putsch as yet another "stab" in Germany's "back." Dohnanyi's secret work with Beck and Oster continued, and soon Admiral Canaris sent him a message: if war came, Canaris wanted him on the Abwehr staff at once.

Meanwhile, Bonhoeffer was finding it almost impossible to continue his ministry in Pomerania, given the ever stricter proscriptions and prohibitions against meeting or even communicating, and given that Confessing Church pastors seemed to be giving in and giving up under the extreme Nazi pressures. Those who were still free were shadowed everywhere, and they knew that every sermon could land them in prison or a concentration camp.* In January 1938 the Gestapo had banned Dietrich from Berlin, an order whose severity the son and parents, planning together, were able to mitigate but not have rescinded—he was allowed to see them but forbidden to attend meetings.

After the closing of Finkenwalde, Dietrich and a handful of other pastors had cobbled together an arrangement whereby he went on supervising a small number of ordinands in a system of "collective pastorates" and they could continue with their apprenticeships. But to manage this he was living like a penniless Gypsy in the little villages and towns of Pomerania, ministering also to the families of dozens of his students whom the Gestapo was persecuting with house searches, interrogations, and arrests. His pastoral letters to the ordinands, composed regularly throughout this difficult period, are superb expositions of what he believed Scripture could teach them—and him—about how the church might function in an honorable and godly way in the midst of malignant chaos.

Dietrich's parents were already worried about the well-being of the Leibholzes, who were trying to eke out a living in England (they were helped there by Bishop Bell, and Eberhard Bethge sent Gert legal tomes into which he could slip German currency[46]); now they were equally concerned for Dietrich's safety. There was also his pending draft: he had to register with local authorities in Pomerania, the first step on the way to induction.

Overall the situation was untenable, and at some level Bonhoeffer knew it—hence the several ambiguous, ambivalent remarks he let drop

---

*I knew this from Confessing pastors in Breslau—I remember their names. –F. S.

about going abroad. Yet he was genuinely committed to his theological work and to his students; for the good of his soul and theirs he felt he must not abandon either. His position as a working pastor seemed to him both more urgent and less possible. In 1936 church and government authorities had allowed him to leave Germany on official church business, and this had given him opportunities to meet with sympathetic clerics abroad to whom he could convey news from the beleaguered Confessing Church holdouts. But he hadn't been allowed out of Germany since February 1937, and the now disabled Confessing Church was effectively beyond the reach of ecumenical assistance.

What if he could arrange for an assignment abroad that the authorities would accept as a temporary alternative to the dreaded army service? When in early 1939 he heard that Reinhold Niebuhr was going to be in Britain, where Dietrich also wanted to see the Leibholzes, he wrote asking Niebuhr if they might talk; some time in America was perhaps not impossible. The Gestapo permitted this trip, and Bonhoeffer, along with Bethge, left for England on March 12. And in England he could also confer with two extraordinary men who were becoming invaluable allies: the saintly George Bell, bishop of Chichester, who had befriended him in 1933 and was dedicated to building international support for the Confessing Church; and a Dutch theologian named Willem Visser 't Hooft, a serene, tireless young man, newly appointed to run the provisional World Council of Churches office in Geneva.

As many of these ecumenical friends knew, Christian churches in other lands were having their own appeasing moments: fascism had alluring aspects for those who saw it as a bulwark against Bolshevism; and the Spanish civil war, now ending in Franco's victory, had further divided the churches. How much the two seeming opposites, Bolshevism and fascism, benefited from each other! At least Pope Pius XI, in his celebrated encyclical *With Burning Sorrow*—written, unusually, in German and addressed to the German bishops and archbishops who read it from their pulpits—had finally spoken out in March 1937 against fascist racial dogmas, however cautiously. (When he died in February 1939 he was succeeded by Cardinal Pacelli, whose papal reign began and continued in controversy, especially concerning his conduct toward Nazi Germany.)

The tempo of decision-making accelerated—as indeed it was doing in the world at large. On March 15, 1939, just after Dietrich arrived in England, the Wehrmacht marched into Prague—not only a violation of the Munich Agreement but a clear signal that Hitler no longer was content merely to "bring home" ethnic Germans outside the nation's borders but was launched on a bid for European supremacy. He could now count on Czechoslovakia's considerable economic and industrial resources for his war machine. And at last "appeasers" began to wake up: two weeks later Great Britain and France countered with a guarantee of Poland's independence; by May, Britain had introduced limited peacetime conscription for the first time in its history.

On April 3 Bonhoeffer along with Gert Leibholz went to see Niebuhr in Sussex. Niebuhr, who had been thinking for some time about what assignments he could find for Bonhoeffer in the United States, quickly recognized the urgency of saving him from immediate military service, and he sent letters to the president of Union Theological Seminary, Henry Sloane Coffin, and other church people in New York asking their help in getting Bonhoeffer a position there as soon as possible. Simultaneously Bonhoeffer's father managed to persuade the army authorities to grant Dietrich's request for a year's leave before being called up. By mid-May he learned that Coffin could arrange an appointment for him to teach at Union during its summer session. On June 2, he and his brother Karl-Friedrich, who was due to give lectures at the University of Chicago, left Berlin together and were soon on the SS *Bremen*, headed for New York.

But Bonhoeffer was torn about what to do—how could he not be? How could he not have asked himself, given the imminence of war: Where lies the path of duty? He had obligations and loyalties on all sides: to his family, his church, his nation, and himself. How could he choose peace and comfort in an alien land while his own was on the brink of war? His diary entries from his time in America express intense, agonizing self-examination. He recorded with surprise his unexpected but anguished *Heimweh* (homesickness), and sensed his duty to return to his brethren and his family. Remarkably, he made no effort to get in touch with German émigrés in New York (except for Felix Gilbert, whom he had known since their days in the same gymnasium class). Dietrich wrote in his diary: "Most pleasant encounter since our time in school. He admires Roosevelt greatly. He explained a lot to me."[47] But Dietrich also recorded his dislike of America: much of its life and culture seemed superficial to him, and he was appalled by the signs of American anti-Semitism. Perhaps he needed to dislike America in order to stiffen his resolve; in the end, he accepted that the grounds for the choice he was to make were unfathomable.

After this intense self-questioning, he decided he must return to Germany as soon as he could. (Chroniclers who celebrate this as a demonstration of selfless Christian bravery might note that his agnostic brother Karl-Friedrich made the same choice, declining a permanent chair in Chicago while Dietrich was explaining his decision to Coffin and the others in New York.) And on July 1 he wrote to his parents in the code they had adopted years before, in which "Uncle Rudi" (Rüdiger Count von der Goltz, the anti-Semitic general) meant "German war moves": "please write Uncle Rudi's birthday to Sabine for me in good time, so that I can, if necessary, send my personal congratulations?" (He hoped to see the Leibholzes in England on his way home.) And within the week he had also written to Niebuhr about his decision:

I have made a mistake in coming to America. I must live through this difficult period of our national history with the Christian people of Germany. I will have no right to participate in the reconstruction of Christian life in Germany after the war if I do not share the trials of this time with my people.... Christians in Germany are going to face the terrible alternative of either willing the defeat of their nation in order that Christian civilization may survive, or willing the victory of their nation and thereby destroying our civilization. I know which of these alternatives I must choose, but I cannot make that choice in security.*

Few Germans were willing to face this "terrible" choice, and still fewer came close to choosing as Dietrich did.

On July 7, the Bonhoeffer brothers sailed back to Europe together. Dietrich was with his students in Pomerania soon after returning to Germany, but a message from his parents told him that Uncle Rudi was faring so poorly that there was no hope for him. And then came a diplomatic revolution: halfhearted Anglo-French efforts to conclude a military alliance with the Soviet Union had stalled, and by August 23 Foreign Minister Ribbentrop was in Moscow to sign the USSR's nonaggression pact with Germany. This was surely the prelude to war with Poland and to Poland's eventual partition. (How quickly the two totalitarian states scuttled their ideological commitments!) Dietrich went back to Berlin: a good part of Pomerania had already become a vast forward operating base for the Wehrmacht, his outpost was very close to what would be the battlefront, and he wanted to be with his parents in Berlin when war came.

---

*Some scholars cite these as Bonhoeffer's own words; in fact, the text is that of Niebuhr's effort, six years later, to set down his recollection of Bonhoeffer's 1939 letter to him, which was lost. See Niebuhr, "The Death of a Martyr," *Christianity and Crisis*, June 25, 1945, pp. 6–7.

In that same month Admiral Canaris summoned Hans von Dohnanyi to the Abwehr. He left the Reichsgericht and Leipzig and, with his family, returned to Berlin, where he became Oster's deputy in the Abwehr—and gained the liberating status of being *u.k. (unabkömmlich)*, indispensable in his present assignment and therefore not subject to conscription. Military counterintelligence had quite a few anti-Hitler plotters in key positions, not just Canaris and Oster, so it was a good place for Dohnanyi to be, even if dangerous, since the Gestapo and SS thought the Abwehr men were "unreliable"; their murderous dislike of their rivals was to cost many resisters their lives. Dohnanyi again had access to restricted materials and now could disguise some of his conspiratorial activities as intelligence work. His main efforts were to help link disparate resistance cells and thus expand the network, hoping to bring the wavering army generals together with civilians of diverse backgrounds.

The strain of the doubled work—serving the criminal regime openly and conspiring against it secretly—was tremendous, and the first especially caused Hans anguish. He found great comfort in sharing with his wife his self-doubts about it while the secret work intensified. And more and more he turned to Dietrich as friend and confidant about the anti-Hitler work, and they tried to see each other at the Bonhoeffers' conveniently remote home in Berlin whenever they could.

And now there was indeed war. Germans, however, showed none of the bellicose enthusiasm for battle that had erupted in August 1914. On September 1 the Wehrmacht invaded Poland, and two days later Britain and France declared war on Germany, but they did not come to their ally's aid; on September 17 the Red Army advanced into Poland from the east, and by the end of the month Poland had virtually ceased to exist.

The Polish campaign was marked from the start by extreme ferocity, by savage plundering and rape, by arbitrary shootings, burning of synagogues, and excesses of cruelty unleashed not only by the Wehrmacht but especially by the SS and police battalions following the army units. Hitler made sure, however, that it was celebrated as a cleanly executed blitzkrieg against Germany's ancient foe. Clever dramatic newsreels glorifying the Wehrmacht's military exploits, shown both at home and abroad, were meant to hearten the Germans and intimidate enemies and neutrals alike. They showed nothing of the rampaging ethnic cleansing and calculated savagery, and nothing was said of the Nazis' ultimate plans to eliminate Poland's elites and reduce the population to illiterate servitude. The Russians faithfully supplied the Wehrmacht with much-needed oil and grain, and Hitler made a "peace offer" to the French and British in October. But even the Chamberlain government refused to consider it.

The onset of war makes church work difficult in any society, and for Germany's Confessing Church pastors in 1939–1940 it became especially risky. In September, Bonhoeffer explored the possibility of becoming an army chaplain. He had so well absorbed the ethic of clandestine resistance to tyranny that he felt no conflict in the idea of ministering to German soldiers. It was at least genuine work on behalf of a genuine community and it would not interfere with—indeed might help—his secret work with Dohnanyi and Oster and the others. When his offer was rejected he returned to what his family called his "life in the forests" of Pomerania. Bonhoeffer recognized there that his prescriptions for living and working together in a Christian community as he had formulated them at Finkenwalde needed to be refreshed and intensified. He composed a little book called *Life Together* that spelled out his austere but reassuring advice on sustaining a Christian life in families and groups, and on churches giving comfort and support to their members—even, or especially, in times of war.

And there was no end in sight to times of war. Even before the

Polish hostilities ceased, Hitler decided that an attack on the West should follow the conquest and demolition of Poland. Most of the Wehrmacht command was far from enthusiastic about his plans for an invasion of the Low Countries and France, as the anti-regime conspirators knew, but Hitler ordered it—first for November 12, then for a later date; it was postponed, canceled, and rescheduled more than a dozen times. Likewise the various plans for Hitler's removal stopped and started up again. And all through the winter months the plotters were putting out feelers to foreign powers, especially England, in the hope of getting reassurances that after a successful putsch the Allies might agree to a "reasonable," that is, nonpunitive, peace. Then in April 1940 a new front opened with Germany's invasion and occupation of Denmark and Norway.

Hans Oster was infuriated by the expansion of the war. In March he had taken the very risky step of assuring a Dutch diplomat friend that he would warn him promptly of the date of any German invasion of neutral Holland; he kept up this contact until the evening of May 9.* Simultaneously he managed, via the conspirators' contacts in the Vatican, to inform the Danish, Norwegian, and British governments of Germany's impending attack on Denmark and Norway.[48] Bonhoeffer was greatly impressed—he met Oster for the first time on Easter Sunday, March 24—appreciating this "treason" as motivated by true patriotism. He, like Dohnanyi and Oster, had left behind the conventional idea of national loyalty to which, notwithstanding Hit-

---

*"On the evening of 9 May the two [Oster and D.J. Sas, the Dutch military attaché] were still together [in Berlin]. They...went into town for dinner—Sas later referred to it as 'more or less a funeral meal'—and then Oster once more stopped at [Wehrmacht headquarters] to check out the latest developments. After twenty minutes Oster returned saying: 'My dear friend, now it is really all over.... The pig has gone off to the Western front.'" Klemens von Klemperer, *German Resistance Against Hitler: The Search for Allies Abroad, 1938–1945* (Oxford University Press, 1992), p. 195.

ler's perversion of their nation's moral order, most frightened, passive Germans still adhered. Oster, risking certain death as a traitor, wanted to act in the interests of a Germany that was resisting tyranny. And he wanted the Allies to know there was a reliable Germany ready to take its part in a post-Hitler Europe.

The brothers-in-law regularly confided in each other during those uneasy months of what in the West was called the Phony War. One evening Hans asked Dietrich what he thought of Jesus's saying that "all they that take the sword shall perish with the sword" (Matthew 26:52). Would that apply to murderers of Hitler? Dietrich said yes, they were subject to that judgment. There was a need for people who would submit to it, fully accepting their own responsibility for their actions.

This nugget of biblical interpretation and moral instruction was the inestimable reassurance that Bonhoeffer gave to Dohnanyi and to Oster. And it corresponded to an evolution in his own experience: he had been an opponent and a resister within the church; now he was going to join their conspiracy against the state—understanding the risks and recognizing the likely punishment. Two years earlier he had told Karl-Friedrich that he was sure the churches were worth making sacrifices for, and though nobody was keen on going to prison, "if it comes to that, then it is a joy, or so I hope, because the cause is worth it."[49] And two years later he was to write, "I do not think that death can take us by surprise now. After what we have been through during the war,...it is we ourselves, and not outward circumstances, who make death what it can be—freely and voluntarily accepted."[50] For Hans, Christine, and Dietrich, the "cause" became a given, an all-encompassing commitment. They had moments of doubt, of course, but decency was the sanction for living this risky double life.

From Pomerania Dietrich regularly wrote to his parents, and sometimes—curtly, cagily—he made known his awareness of important developments. For example, in late February 1940 a letter said, "About the dissolution of Pomeranian insane asylums Papa will have heard extensively."[51] Indeed Dr. Bonhoeffer had. Top secret "euthanasia actions" against asylum patients and others had started in Pomerania months before, when the Interior Ministry circulated a decree compelling all physicians, nurses, and midwives to report newborn infants and small children who showed signs of severe mental or physical disability; parents of older children with disabilities were encouraged to bring them to certain designated "pediatric clinics." (The decree was backdated to September 1, 1939, to make it look like a "wartime measure.")

By January 1940, functionaries were removing patients chosen for the program on the basis of these reports—disabled, deranged, or permanently ill men, women, and children judged to be incurable, hence "unworthy of life," in Hitler's phrase—and transporting them to one of six "clinics" equipped with instruments of death, including gas chambers. Dr. Bonhoeffer knew about one of these killing centers (Zuchthaus Brandenburg). Dietrich met repeatedly with two pastors, Paul Braune and Friedrich von Bodelschwingh, who knew firsthand about this horrifying subject, concerned as they were about patients in their hospitals and asylums who had been taken away and now had disappeared (their eventual obituaries had been disturbingly strange). Dr. Bonhoeffer confronted his successor at the Charité, Max de Crinis, over the whole issue and was shocked by the latter's mendacity about it; de Crinis continued his commanding involvement with the murderous program.*

The practice of liquidating disabled patients had also spread back into Germany from occupied Poland, where SS men following at the

---

*De Crinis became medical director of the Ministry of Education in 1941. On May 1, 1945, he killed first his family with potassium cyanide and then himself with a cyanide tablet.

rear of the Wehrmacht had been not only annihilating Jews and Poles but clearing out hospitals and asylums by shooting the inmates. Pomerania's enthusiastic Gauleiter in January 1940 likewise ordered the evacuation of psychiatric hospitals and nursing homes in five districts. The patients were transported elsewhere to be either shot or gassed; and it was noted that this made room for wounded SS men returning from the front and lessened the pressures of food scarcity in the hospitals.

Dohnanyi, too, met with the pastors and helped them to compose a memorandum specifying explicit details of this "top secret" project and stressing its lawless disregard "of the inviolability of the person." With his help they submitted this document to Franz Gürtner, who, like other cabinet members, had been kept in the dark about the murderous program. (It was top secret within the government yet could not easily be kept under wraps, since so many doctors and bureaucrats had to falsify official records in order to have them show that the victims had died of natural causes. Whispers abounded, and thousands of people saw the gray buses transporting the victims to the killing centers.)

In July 1940 Hans arranged to have the pastors meet privately with Gürtner at his home, along with (at Dr. Bonhoeffer's suggestion) a well-known colleague, Ferdinand Sauerbruch, Germany's most renowned surgeon and the director of the Charité. Gürtner was shocked by what the three men told him and shocked that he hadn't known about it. He tried to intervene, but he was powerless to stop the ongoing slaughter. So the pastors delivered a further protest, this time to Hans-Heinrich Lammers, the chief of Hitler's chancellery office, which had initiated the decrees setting forth the program, asking formally that the "actions" be terminated; Hitler's response was to order their continuation—"to be executed decently." (The Gestapo quickly arrested Braune and released him only in late October 1940.)

A full year later, in August 1941, Hitler finally decreed an end to the "euthanasia actions"—but that was only after the influential Roman Catholic Archbishop Clemens Count von Galen of Münster had denounced the program from his pulpit; his impassioned sermon on this subject was widely circulated, and he sent the text to Hitler himself. Yet by then almost 90,000 German men, women, and children had been murdered.[52] Clandestine Nazi killings of the lame, the halt, and the blind continued in one way or another until Germany's defeat.

During the early wartime seasons, and once Pomerania's remote, sparsely populated districts were outside the area of military operations, Dietrich and his friend Eberhard Bethge were managing, against all odds, to continue to minister to a few parishes and to instruct a few more ordinands there. In the exceptionally cold winter that year, it was physically harsh: in a letter of January 1940 to his brother Karl-Friedrich, Dietrich wrote, "We sit here worrying about coal, and without oil, so that we have to use candles for as long as they last. We are completely cut off from the city." But he came to appreciate the spiritual isolation. A few weeks later, he told his parents, "Life in the country, especially in times like these, is much more dignified for people than in the city."[53]

Not only were the physical circumstances difficult, but Dietrich knew that the young pastors-to-be whom he was mentoring were in an unbearable situation—caught between doing their work as they thought they should, which the authorities deemed illegal, or compromising their integrity by joining a Nazi-approved congregation, which at least allowed them to carry out basic pastoral duties. In this administrative, ethical, and civic chaos, Dietrich conveyed to his ordinands the centrality of the question that had always concerned him: What *is* a church, in the end? What do the Gospels tell us, what does Jesus say, how did the early church imagine itself? What is Luther's position on this, what should a German pastor believe today? In letters and sermons, and in countless long conversations with his students, Dietrich worked to clarify his theological and practical views on these issues.

But the Gestapo had Dietrich in its sights. In mid-July 1940, its office in Königsberg warned the Reich Central Security Office (RSHA) that "Bonnhofer" [*sic*] was speaking to various Confessing Church groups; that he belonged to the circle around Niemöller and had mentioned meeting the archbishop of Canterbury; that in a discussion he had asserted that Polish prisoners, once disarmed, were no longer "enemies" and that women and children never were. More: that the path to salvation was narrow, open only to the few and only through the Confessing Church; that the German masses were marching on a different path to perdition. Further, though he claimed to have a domicile in Schluwe (by which they meant Schlawe, the ancient Pomeranian town where indeed Bonhoeffer had established residence and registered with the police), he was actually traveling all across the Reich, speaking everywhere.[54]

When in August the RSHA banned Bonhoeffer from public speaking anywhere in Germany because of what it charged was his defeatist (*volkszersetzende*) activity, he protested the prohibition's insulting terms. At times he wanted to believe that the German "state" could not be continually deaf to reason, that appeals might be heard and some illegalities rescinded. In September he wrote to the RSHA repudiating the charge; it could hardly be applied, he said in good Bonhoeffer high dudgeon, given

> my entire outlook, attitude, my work as well as my background....
> I am proud to belong to a family that has rendered outstanding service to the German people and nation for generations....

[Names of ancestral generals, artists, and scholars in high office followed.] My brothers and brothers-in-law serve in high
government positions, and one of my brothers was killed in the
First World War.... In conscious affirmation of this spiritual
legacy and the moral position [*Haltung*] of my family I cannot
accept this charge.[55]

He asked for an interview, signed the letter "Heil Hitler," and received no answer. The ban was never revoked.

The Wehrmacht's attack in the West on May 10, 1940, proved to be
a brilliant success, against all the warnings of the generals. (Field
Marshal Erich von Manstein had devised the Germans' daring thrust
through the Ardennes, but Hitler of course took the credit for it.) In
June 1940 Paris fell—a once unimaginable revenge for the defeat of
1918. Most Germans were jubilant, and even some critics were awed.
Hitler was at the height of his power and popularity. Quickly enough
—and not just in France—appeasement turned into collaboration;
Europe seemed done for. But a formidable foe had emerged—the new
British prime minister, Winston Churchill—and over the summer the
Royal Air Force, in the ferocious Battle of Britain, foiled Hitler's in-
tention to invade the British Isles. Hitler fell back on his next and
boldest move: soon would come an attack on the Soviet Union.

During that dark summer after the fall of France, Dietrich and
Hans were in closest collaboration—and not just in their efforts to
stop the euthanasia program. In August Dietrich joined a meeting in
the Bonhoeffers' Berlin home with Hans, Oster, and another Abwehr
conspirator. And a few months later, Hans and Oster were able to
put Dietrich's apprehensions about army service to rest: they would
arrange for him to be made a civilian *V-Mann* (*Verbindungsmann*,
liaison person) with the Abwehr, which would, the official explana-

tion ran, profit from his extensive international contacts. Though never a formal member of the Abwehr, as a *V-Mann* Dietrich received *u.k.* status in early 1941—all the more important now that the Nazis were drafting as many Confessing Church pastors as they could and sending them off to the front. (At Dietrich's request Hans later managed to get *u.k.* status for several of Dietrich's closest associates.) Thus did Bonhoeffer begin his ostensible work for the military arm of the Nazi regime—months after the fall of Norway and the fall of France—when Hitler's triumph was at its zenith and most Germans were jubilantly following their Führer. Never had Nietzsche's warning been more apt: "A great victory is a great danger."

To balance the contradictory obligations of being a pastor in a nation at war and doing conspiratorial work against the regime required prudence and inestimable courage, especially since Himmler's RSHA was ever more suspicious of wandering pastors and of anyone with a connection to Canaris and his people in the Abwehr. On top of that, for the first time in more than a decade Bonhoeffer had no formal church affiliation or stipend. In truth the Confessing Church was in tatters, and he was only scraping by with minor assignments from the Old Prussian Union's Council of Brethren. In any case preaching to congregations who were exulting about Germany's victory over France, or discussing the Gospel with patriotic army chaplains, created hideous spiritual conflicts.

Since the Gestapo had the Abwehr under heightened scrutiny, in October Oster and Canaris sent Dietrich off to its Munich office and its perhaps relative safety; there they instructed him to contact Josef Müller, a well-connected and devoted Catholic lawyer who had been working with the Abwehr resisters for some time (Dietrich had already met him in Berlin) and who had well-established relations with Vatican diplomats. General Beck thought that Müller might assist in gaining that perennially hoped-for goal: Britain's agreement on reasonable peace terms for Germany once Hitler was gone. Thus Müller was repeatedly dispatched to the Vatican in anticipation that its diplomats could establish contacts with the British—an effort in which it was hoped that Dietrich, with his useful English contacts, could be helpful. Hans, on repeated trips to Italy, did his part as well. It was delicate, of course: the Vatican diplomats would be seriously compromised if their connections to the German resistance became known.

Helmuth James Count von Moltke—a dashing and fearless member of a Prussian clan famous for the field marshal who planned and led Bismarck's wars, for other luminaries, and for its broad intellectual interests—was another anti-Nazi lawyer in the Abwehr and also deeply involved in these plans. Moltke also had been assembling an extensive group of resisters to ponder a better political and social order in Germany after Hitler. Though he loathed the regime, he hesitated on moral and rational grounds to approve of the idea of Hitler's murder, as one of those who feared that if a punitive peace followed it, Germans might all too readily succumb once more to a stab-in-the-back legend. To conspire knowing that your countrymen would think you traitorous was a special burden on certain of the German resisters like Moltke; the record of their nation's past, with all its distortions, haunted these people.

But Dohnanyi and Moltke continued under harrowing conditions to forge links among the various groups of resisters—from the still mostly aristocratic Wehrmacht officers on the eastern front to experienced lawyers in Berlin with international contacts (Klaus Bonhoeffer, his friends the brothers Hans and Otto John, and Justus Delbrück were already among them, as well as Lieutenant Fabian von Schlabrendorff, a liaison between the lawyers in Berlin and the officers in the east) and the few remaining Socialist and Communist Party leaders (for example the brave Socialists Julius Leber and Wilhelm Leuschner, both already veterans of Hitler's concentration camps). It was almost miraculous that these men managed to link up at all, when the world was full of informers and police surveillance was total, when they had no safety in phones or mail and no protection against invisible Gestapo microphones. Moltke's estate in Silesia, Kreisau, became a meeting place where resisters could ponder their plans for a post-Hitler Germany.

During his Bavarian interlude, Bonhoeffer was a guest for several months, thanks to Müller, at the Benedictine monastery at Ettal. In this calm setting he could focus again on his theological work; he drafted and composed sections of a book on ethics there. This was of surpassing importance to him. Then in February 1941 he was ordered on his first Abwehr trip abroad—to Switzerland. On being asked by a border guard who his Swiss "guarantor" was—a question he hadn't expected—Bonhoeffer impulsively gave the name of Karl Barth, whom the guard telephoned just to make sure; he then proceeded to Zurich where among other things he met with another resister, H. B. Gisevius, Germany's vice-consul there. Gisevius had a hostile view of him, motivated in part by malicious jealousy, wanting no one to interfere with his self-appointed role as chief conspirator in residence. (After the war he ungenerously besmirched some of the resisters' names, notably Dohnanyi's, in his testimony at the Nuremberg trials.)

After fulfilling various Abwehr chores, Dietrich went to Basel to reassure Barth in person that despite his traveling in neutral Switzerland with official German papers he was still actively involved in oppositional work in the church; he also told Barth in confidence about his new responsibilities in the anti-Hitler plots. About these Barth feared, plausibly enough, that the generals, even in their anti-Hitler mode, might have excessive expectations about expanded borders for a post-Hitler Germany, and he worried that his young friend was naive about this difficulty. Lastly Dietrich saw Visser 't Hooft in Geneva; he was able to assure him—and, through him, the many other ecumenical figures who knew of the German resistance—about the resilience and strength of the anti-Hitler groups.

In the spring of 1941, Hans and Christine bought a house in Sakrow, a Berlin suburb near Potsdam; it was meant to be a peaceful home for the family—and at least it was far from the British air attacks on the capital. (Later in the war their children were sent to school in Ettal, since the air raids made for intermittent hazards to their schooling in Berlin.) But the family was to have no peace.

Dietrich Bonhoeffer's parents,
Dr. Karl Bonhoeffer and Paula von Hase Bonhoeffer

Hans von Dohnanyi's parents,
Ernst von Dohnányi and Elisabeth Kunwald von Dohnányi

The Bonhoeffer family on vacation in 1907,
a postcard for friends sent to Fritz Stern's grandparents

Hans von Dohnanyi and Christine Bonhoeffer
at the time of their engagement in 1927

Dietrich Bonhoeffer in 1932,
at an ecumenical conference in Gland, Switzerland

Franz Gürtner,
Germany's Minister of Justice,
1932–1941

Brigadier General Hans Oster,
deputy to Admiral Wilhelm Canaris,
director of the Abwehr, 1933–1943

General Ludwig Beck,
Army Chief of Staff, 1935–1938

George Bell, Bishop of Chichester, 1929–1958 (left),
with Pastor Franz Hildebrandt (middle), a close friend of Bonhoeffer's,
in front of St. Martin's in the Field, London, July 1941

Pastor Martin Niemöller

Dietrich Bonhoeffer in the courtyard of the military interrogation jail
at Berlin-Tegel, July 1944

Sketches made by Hans von Dohnanyi
during his imprisonment in 1943 and 1944.
Clockwise from top left: his tormenting interrogator Manfred Roeder,
a self-portrait, a nosegay of flowers for Christine on her birthday in 1944,
Christine having an afternoon nap, and his daughter Bärbel for Christine
on her birthday in 1943.

Karl and Paula Bonhoeffer, after World War II

IV

FROM THE VERY first, Operation Barbarossa, Germany's audacious attack on the Soviet Union in June 1941—across a front of over a thousand miles, involving between four and five million troops—envisioned unbounded barbarism, with no restraints of law or conscience. The German commanders were given Hitler's order to kill all Soviet "commissars" weeks before the invasion actually began just before dawn on June 22, and they had further license to kill people identified as "thoroughly bolshevized as active representatives of the Bolshevist ideology." Moltke and Dohnanyi were among those who knew about the horrendous crimes that had already been committed in Poland, and they knew or intuited that the Wehrmacht's highest commanders knew about and allowed the killings now being carried out in newly occupied areas to the rear of the eastern front. They were shaken to the core to learn about this alarming expansion of the atrocities perpetrated—the murder of Jewish men, women, and children (600,000 of them by March 1942), the systematic starvation of Soviet prisoners, the killing of Russian officers. No "clean" Wehrmacht for them!

Germans were anxious about this huge expansion of the war, and the regime watched public morale closely; Hitler and Goebbels sensed the growing unease. In October 1941, while the Wehrmacht was still making huge advances in the east, Hitler was persuaded to give a rousing speech at the Sportspalast in which he launched the myth that Germany had been forced into a preemptive war in order to protect itself, indeed all Europe, against an imminent attack by the Soviet Union (this myth is still peddled in right-wing German circles).

The utter inhumanity of the war on the eastern front led to grumbling and protests in the Wehrmacht against Hitler's "Commissar Order," so in May 1942 he rescinded it and never reissued it. The slaughter continued, however, and Wehrmacht officers also had to obey Hitler's order that in the event of any German retreat the Red Army should reclaim nothing but scorched earth. But many of them knew that scorched earth, murder, and starvation only strengthened Soviet resistance and alienated people who might otherwise be anti-Russian collaborators, for example Ukrainians. When the conspirators tried to persuade top generals to join in the plan to remove Hitler, they got nowhere, yet while the generals balked some officers of lower rank, younger men who were directly exposed to the mass murders, rallied to them, recognizing that hundreds of thousands of German soldiers were sacrificing themselves in vain while the German people were incurring ever more shame and guilt.[56]

And the terror at home was worsening. With most of Europe under their control, the Nazis readied new coordinated policies against Jews in Germany. In January 1939, at the ritualized celebration of his accession to power—when Germany had still been at peace—Hitler had prophesied before the world that in case of another war international Jewry would be extinguished. And as Dietrich had reported, sporadic deportations of German Jews had already begun in October 1940, when Jews from Baden were rounded up and sent to Gurs, a concentration camp in southern France. Dietrich alerted Hans to the fate of "non-Aryan" friends there; he found ways to send supplies to a few of the victims, including Emil Perels, father of his close friend

Justus Perels, a lawyer working for the Old Prussian Union's Council of Brethren and giving invaluable assistance to its embattled clergy.

In December 1941 the situation on the eastern front changed dramatically. The Wehrmacht's advance into Russia over the summer had been swift—German forces captured Minsk by July and Smolensk by August—but harrowing conditions and reversals during the autumn, some caused by Hitler's own wayward decisions, put the German forces in harshly exposed positions without adequate support or supplies, let alone winter clothing. The setbacks on one sector of the front led Hitler to remove Field Marshal Gerd von Rundstedt from command, while farther north the Wehrmacht advanced as far as the suburbs of Moscow. But there the exhausted German troops faced a dramatically successful counterattack launched on December 5 by the supposedly vanquished Red Army—it was Germany's first major defeat. Hitler had ignored among other things the predictable effects of the Russian winter.*

Then on December 7 Japanese planes attacked Pearl Harbor, bringing the United States into the war (it had been edging in this direction for months). Hitler, driven by hatred of Franklin Roosevelt, whom he thought of as a front for Judeo-Bolshevik forces, decided to declare war on the United States; once again, as in 1917, German leaders underestimated America's potential power. Germany, Italy, and Japan proclaimed their united will—that is, they eliminated the possibility that any of them might negotiate a separate peace. And in a show of power Hitler sacked some more generals, including, on Christmas Day, the panzer commander Heinz Guderian (he did not reinstate him until 1943), and dismissed the ailing, disheartened Field

---

*In a well-researched television documentary about those days, German soldiers complained at length about their having suffered under the subzero conditions. A woman from Moscow who had lived through that period said simply, "It was cold for us, too."

Marshal Walther von Brauchitsch as chief of staff and took over the position himself—a move that made any plan to remove him both more urgent and more difficult.

In September 1941 the Nazis decreed that Germans designated as Jewish (including *Mischlinge*—only partly Jewish people) must wear the yellow star on their outer clothes.* In the same weeks, Heinrich Himmler and his deputy Reinhard Heydrich coordinated "the final solution" with all the relevant government ministries (it was formally ratified at the Wannsee Conference in January 1942). And Himmler ordered the deportation of Jews from Berlin and other cities to unspecified points in the east; these took place—in full daylight (in Berlin, from the railroad station in Grunewald). Did no one notice? At the same time, Himmler forbade Jews from emigrating: the Nazis meant the Jews to be trapped. The policy of extrusion was becoming a policy of extinction.

Within a few weeks Bonhoeffer and Justus Perels had assembled reports on the deportations for Dohnanyi, who showed them to Hans Oster and to General Beck in the hope that they could either persuade the Wehrmacht commanders to intervene or accelerate their anti-Hitler plans.[57] Hans also learned that Fritz Arnold and Julius Fliess, two lawyers—severely wounded and decorated veterans of the Great War—to whom in 1934 he (along with Gürtner) had promised protection, now faced further demotion and deportation. With an official protest from the Wehrmacht's high command he could obtain a temporary delay of deportation for Fliess, but Arnold was in equal danger. Hans—himself under the closest surveillance—was nonetheless resolved to help. Christine remembered him saying, "I will not

---

*Visser 't Hooft noted in November that in various Protestant churches in Berlin "converted Jews wearing their stars are regularly taking part in communion services." *Dietrich Bonhoeffer Werke*, Vol. 16, p. 215.

let anything happen to these men to whom I gave my promise... only over my dead body."[58] While at the Ministry of Justice, Dohnanyi had helped Martin Niemöller and other Confessing Church pastors in any number of ways and had become their "man to turn to." He continued this *Privatpraxis* after the war began and he was in the Abwehr; even "non-Aryans" came to his office there for advice. And he was there when Dietrich let him know about the deportation threat to Charlotte Friedenthal,* for many years an active membee of the Confessing Church and most recently employed by Pastor Heinrich Grüber, in Berlin, who was doing a great deal to help "non-Aryan" Christians. (Grüber himself had been arrested and sent to a concentration camp in December 1940.)

After anguished reflection on these cases, Hans hit on an ingenious, audacious plan that would allow the two lawyers and a few other "non-Aryans" to escape deportation and death: with Canaris's and Oster's support, they would be appointed as "confidential agents" for the Abwehr so that they would be permitted to reach Switzerland, with the understanding that they would be dispatched from there to South America to spy for the Reich. This immensely complicated effort to save the seven (the list grew to fourteen), most of them Confessing Church members, became known as Operation 7.†

The obstacles were many. The Swiss, then at the height of their

---

*A relative of mine by marriage—F. S.

†The drama had its beginnings in an Abwehr policy of sending Jews—preferably of the German nationalistic type—abroad as spies; the earliest successes were in Harbin, China. The presumption was that they could more easily gain access to good intelligence sources. Dohnanyi was also marginally involved in another Abwehr effort that, in 1940, helped Rabbi Menachem Mendel Schneersohn, later to become head of the Chabad movement of Hasidic Jews, to leave Paris, where he had sought refuge in 1933, and to reach safety in New York in 1941. For a most carefully researched account of Hans's direction of this amazing enterprise, see Meyer, *Unternehmen Sieben.*

anti-Semitic, anti-refugee policy, had to grant visas. Bonhoeffer enlisted Alphons Koechlin, president of the Swiss Evangelical Kirchenbund, and Karl Barth helped as well. Dohnanyi also insisted that the so-called agents, once in Switzerland, should receive $100,000 from German reserves, in compensation for the goods they'd had to leave behind and to demonstrate that they had no need of Swiss public funds. Of course the Gestapo had to consent to this remarkable venture, which it did. When Dohnanyi told Arnold the details of the plan, Arnold recoiled in astonishment: he would never spy for the Nazi regime! Dohnanyi quickly persuaded him that the plan required this as a ruse.* With Dohnanyi himself in Switzerland, carrying the needed funds, Friedenthal crossed the border on September 5, 1942, the others shortly after.

This extraordinary undertaking, a miracle for the fourteen people who were saved, was a monumental risk for Hans. Under Gestapo surveillance for six years and with jealous enemies within the Abwehr, he had put himself in still greater jeopardy. His enemies hoped they could catch him; projecting their own baseness on him, they presumed that no one would undertake such work without trying to enrich himself. They speculated that perhaps "currency violations" could be discovered that would prove his undoing. They launched all manner of investigations.

Roughly fifty years later, and with Operation 7 very much in mind, Hans's son Klaus wrote of his father: "He was an astute conspirator.... But above all, he was a sensitive person [*Mensch*] with an infallible sense for justice and injustice."[59]

---

*It is odd to think that Hitler might have contributed to this plan. In June 1942, when an Abwehr sabotage effort in the United States collapsed, Hitler upbraided Admiral Canaris for having sent incompetent agents to do the work. In the future, he shouted, "take criminals or Jews." Meyer, *Unternehmen Sieben*, p. 256.

In the spring of 1942 the Abwehr dispatched both Bonhoeffer and Moltke to Norway, but separately, to assess the security situation in this occupied nation. Both men knew that Vidkun Quisling's collaborationist government had arrested Bishop Eivind Berggrav, primate of Norway's Lutheran Church, which was organizing widespread resistance against the German occupation. The overt aim of both men was to gauge the effect this opposition was having on the German forces and to instruct the German command that the policy toward Bishop Berggrav should be respectful and not so harsh (though neither Bonhoeffer nor Moltke knew this, Himmler's supervening order was in fact to release Berggrav immediately). Their covert aim was of course to make a connection with this eminent fellow resister and greatly admired ecumenical church leader, and to signal their support to the resisters. Berggrav had been sent to a concentration camp on April 9, and he was released from it a week later (though kept in detention for the rest of the war). But another drama of the Norwegian episode lies in the meeting of two exceptional Germans on the ship to Norway: both radical enemies of the Nazi regime, both profoundly devout Christians, both working for the Abwehr, who were separated by experience, by temperamental differences, and by their disagreement about the need to kill Hitler, which Moltke opposed but Bonhoeffer had come to believe was necessary.

Dietrich had learned that Bishop George Bell was going to be in Sweden for an ecumenical meeting at about this time, and he managed to fly to Stockholm to see him. He asked Bell, who was stunned to see him in Sweden at this point in the war, if he and his colleagues might win some reassurance from Churchill's government about what its response would be if an anti-Hitler coup were to succeed in Berlin. Bell drew up a memo for the Foreign Office and Foreign Secretary Anthony Eden summarizing his conversations with Bonhoeffer. Bonhoeffer's purpose, it said, had been to inform him of "the strong organized opposition" to Hitler, and its determination to destroy the entire Hitler regime and install a new government; this post-Hitler government would renounce aggression and immediately "repeal the Nuremberg Laws, [seek] cooperation in the international settlement of Jewish problems," and, in stages, withdraw all German troops from occupied countries. It would also assist in establishing economic interdependence among the European nations, including "a Free Polish and a Free Czech Nation," and pledge to support the formation of a European army, of which a German army would be a part. The question then was whether the Allies would agree to negotiate with such a new government. Later in the summer the conspirators learned that Eden refused to entertain Bishop Bell's question or go beyond what he had already said.* This British response, understandable for many reasons, continues to arouse great controversy among historians. And still worse for the resisters, at the Casablanca Conference in January 1943, Roosevelt and Churchill proclaimed the policy of insisting on Germany's "unconditional surrender."

Then, also in early 1943, the Wehrmacht's seemingly unstoppable march *was* finally stopped. On January 31, General Friedrich Paulus, commander of the decimated, encircled German army in Stalingrad, after months of brutal battle there and against Hitler's specific orders, surrendered to the Red Army; hundreds of thousands of German soldiers had died and more than a million Soviet troops; the

---

*We now know of exchanges within the Foreign Office and of Eden's response to Bell in July and August, saying inter alia that the obviously endangered German opposition had "given little evidence of their existence." The English thought they needed to follow the example of the "oppressed peoples of Europe in running risks." The Foreign Office's tone is caught in a note signed by W. Strang: "The Bishop of Chichester and his like have learnt nothing from the two German wars and are now busily, in all innocence, tearing to lay the foundations of a third." To which was penned: "I agree, AE, July 12." *Dietrich Bonhoeffer Werke*, Vol. 16, pp. 327–338.

roughly 110,000 German soldiers remaining there, including twenty-two generals, were taken prisoner (of whom only five thousand returned to Germany after the war).

On hearing of this humiliating defeat, Hitler flew into a rage. But the rout had to be acknowledged: three days of national mourning were ordered in early February.* And there was equally bad news on other fronts. Earlier, in November 1942, British forces had defeated General Erwin Rommel's Africa Corps at El Alamein and Allied forces had landed in Morocco (in retaliation for which Hitler ordered the occupation of Vichy France); those Allied armies were now virtually clearing North Africa, with tens of thousands of German and even more Italian troops surrendering. More German defeats followed.

The surrender at Stalingrad stunned the Germans, who were coming to realize the dimensions of the disaster and the scope of their losses. When, a few weeks later, Goebbels defiantly proclaimed the certitude of victory in a "total war," his speech hardly achieved its goal of raising morale. The regime, ever watchful of the public mood, realized the depth of unease and suspicion. Already in the autumn of 1942, Arvid Harnack (a nephew of the great historian) and his American wife, Mildred, had been arrested and accused of spying for the Soviet Union; the opposition group of which they were a part, which the Gestapo called the Red Orchestra, had members all over Germany. The prosecutor on the case, Manfred Roeder, had seen to it that they were summarily "tried" and then hanged on December 22. (Roeder, known for his vile brutality, was a special favorite of Göring's.) And the White Rose, an oppositional student group at the

---

*Hitler was known to be callously indifferent to German suffering. The special train that took him back and forth between his East Prussian headquarters and the eastern front once encountered a train returning from the front filled with wounded and exhausted soldiers; Hitler ordered his blinds to be lowered. See Ian Kershaw, *Hitler: 1936–1945: Nemesis* (Norton, 2000), p. 565.

University of Munich, had been gaining support and new adherents since the summer of 1942; now, after the nightmare of Stalingrad and on the very day that Goebbels gave his truculent speech, it distributed leaflets calling for an end to the Nazi horrors. The leaders of this group were rounded up that very day, quickly tried in the Peoples' Court before its newly appointed chief, the savage Roland Freisler, and guillotined four days later. For the Nazis, ruthlessness was the only response to internal threats. The resisters vowed to continue their efforts to remove Hitler in order to save what could be saved— for Germans and for their victims, most especially for Jews.

As winter closed in, Bonhoeffer composed for his family, and for Dohnanyi, Oster, and Bethge, a Christmas and New Year's greeting, "Nach Zehn Jahren" ("After Ten Years"), which he read to his family during their Christmas celebrations. He wanted, he told them, to offer an "accounting of some of the shared experience and insight that have been forced upon us in these times" and "conclusions about human experience...that have been reached together in a circle of like-minded people."

Dietrich's dramatic Christmas essay was an unsparing assessment of Germans and their conduct over the previous decade—when, as he wrote, "the huge masquerade of evil has thrown all ethical concepts into confusion,...[when] few have been spared the experience of being betrayed," when Germans who knew all too well the need for obedience "did not reckon with the fact that [it] could be misused in the service of evil." How was one to function in such a world, and what would happen next? And what were the moral consequences of living a deceptive, clandestine life? "Will our inner strength to resist what has been forced on us have remained strong enough, and our honesty with ourselves blunt enough, to find our way back to simplicity and honesty?... Are we still of any use?" Here was a theme—

and many questions—that never left him, as his later letters from prison eloquently attested.

Bonhoeffer made no mention in his essay of the German government or the war, no allusion to subterfuge or doctrinal dispute, but it is suffused with a deep wisdom about all these aspects of the tragedy the German people were bringing upon themselves. He thought that for various reasons having to do with their unique political history, Germans lacked "civil courage" and had put in its place either an "irresponsible lack of scruples" or "self-tormenting scruples that never led to action." Sometimes they fled "from public altercation into the sanctuary of private *virtuousness*," he wrote. "But anyone who does this must shut his mouth and his eyes to the injustice around him. Only at the cost of self-deception can he keep himself pure from the contamination arising from responsible action." Or else the Germans showed a kind of desperate, self-congratulatory bravery in the face of likely defeat. But this was a false bravery, for it did not dare to look into the future and cared only for the present; it could only lead to further desperation.

Both these responses showed that Germans had forsaken something fundamental: they could not see "the need for free and responsible action" even, or especially, when it went against orders and authority. And free and responsible action was precisely what was needed to safeguard the future. "The ultimately responsible question is not how I extricate myself heroically from a situation but how a coming generation is to go on living."[60]

Dietrich's courage to act freely and responsibly—an attribute he shared with his siblings and their spouses—was at the heart of the Bonhoeffer ethic. In the midst of this terrible war and the increasing chaos and destruction afflicting their lives in Berlin, they did not lose sight of it, nor did they ever forget that millions of people were suffering more than they. It was the miserable lack among Germans of their kind of active decency—modest, practical, and gallant—that brought them and their country down. Hans had written to the Leibholzes, "Our solidarity as brothers and sisters, and with our parents, is as strong as ever, so we can be sure of overcoming the difficulties of these violent times."[61] Family and, for some of them, an ever stronger inner sense of Christian faith steeled these brave people; Hans avowed for all of them that they simply thought they should continue "on the path a decent person inevitably takes." No Bonhoeffer or Dohnanyi tolerated talk of heroism or martyrdom.

During this extraordinary year, Dietrich had a transformative experience of a very different kind: he fell in love with the granddaughter of a splendid old lady in East Prussia with whom he had become friends. He had met Maria von Wedemeyer several times when she was a girl, and then was seriously smitten in June 1942. She was by then eighteen—and quite unaware of Dietrich's feelings for her. Tragedy brought them together in August, with the news first of her father's death in the early weeks of the battle at Stalingrad, and then in October the death of her older brother Max, also in the east. (Years before, Dietrich as pastor had confirmed him.) Soon Maria's mother, devastated by this double loss, learned from her mother, Dietrich's friend, that his love of Maria was more than merely pastoral. She told him not to come to Max's funeral and not to press his suit, or at any rate not yet, for she believed her distraught daughter was in no condition to take so momentous a step as a betrothal to a man so much older than she; she asked them both to wait for a year.

On January 13, 1943, however, Maria wrote to Dietrich, "Knowing from experience how well you understand me, I'm now emboldened to write to you, even though I've really no right whatever to answer a question which you have never asked me. With all my happy heart I can now say yes."[62] Dietrich, overjoyed, was ready to shower her with fervent letters, but she then imposed a six-month ban on correspondence. Still, they both considered January 13 the date of their engagement, and so informed their families.

For Dohnanyi and his fellow resisters, thoughts were on sterner stuff. They were set on implementing the next planned coup; they hoped that the disaster at Stalingrad might have convinced more Germans of the necessity of removing the Führer. By late February 1943 Oster and General Friedrich Olbricht in Berlin had completed plans for a putsch that would start with the death of Hitler on the eastern front and include military officers in Berlin and several other strategically key cities seizing power. Early in March their message was sent to fellow conspirators in the east: "We are ready; it is time for the flash." On the evening of March 12 Dohnanyi and Admiral Canaris left together for Smolensk, where they knew Hitler was going to be visiting troops. On the plane to Smolensk, Hans hid the small British-made bomb they had brought with them by sitting on it, and when they arrived, he handed it off to Colonel Henning von Tresckow; the plan was for Tresckow to get the device onto the plane that would take Hitler back to his East Prussian headquarters; it would blow up the plane half an hour after its departure.[63]

The next afternoon Tresckow was able to get the device onto the plane, disguised as two gift bottles of Cointreau, and the Führer departed. But the mechanism didn't function, probably because of extreme cold in the plane's fuselage, and Hitler arrived at his headquarters unscathed. (There Fabian von Schlabrendorff, Tresckow's adjutant and a fellow conspirator, with characteristic sangfroid managed the following morning to exchange the unexploded and still-dangerous bomb for actual triple sec.) And on March 21 another assassination attempt organized by more or less the same people miscarried because of last-minute changes in Hitler's schedule. Neither the SS nor the Gestapo knew of these two failed attempts on Hitler's life.

Ten days later, a full gathering of the Bonhoeffer family took place in Berlin on the occasion of Dr. Karl Bonhoeffer's seventy-fifth birthday. They could not know that this festive event, with its celebratory music and family tenderness, would be their last together. The still-robust Geheimrat Bonhoeffer, now retired but still seeing patients, was cheerfully feted by his children, grandchildren, nephews, and nieces. (Paula's cousin Paul von Hase, a Wehrmacht officer who was now military commander of Berlin, came too. When he appeared in full uniform, Dr. Bonhoeffer cheerfully reproached him and sent him home to dress more appropriately for a family party.) The few friends and neighbors who came included Dr. Bonhoeffer's colleague Professor Sauerbruch, who had just successfully operated on Canaris.* A most curious note was struck by a formal birthday message from Hitler announcing that he was bestowing on Dr. Bonhoeffer the Goethe Medal for Art and Science. The message may have jolted the family, but they knew that the Nazis honored and dishonored with equal abandon.

At the very same time, the Nazis' top security officers had decided they must move against some of the suspected "traitors" in the Abwehr. Sufficient evidence was missing, but they acted anyway: they planned the arrests of Hans, Christine, Dietrich, and, simultaneously, Josef Müller and his wife on allegations of treason as well as "currency violations" in connection with Operation 7. With the express approval of Field Marshal Keitel for the Wehrmacht and Himmler for the SS, their cases went forward and on April 3 were placed in the hands of Manfred Roeder, who on April 5 arrested Hans in his office, then had Christine and Dietrich arrested, too. Dohnanyi and

---

*Sauerbruch's conduct in the Third Reich offers a striking example of the way some eminent Germans behaved: making public accommodations so as to demonstrate loyalty, remain at one's post, and escape persecution, while showing private decency so that at least some self-respect could be preserved.

Müller, arrested in Munich with his wife, were taken secretly to the prison for military officers in Berlin, their wives to the women's prison in Charlottenburg, Dietrich to a prison in Tegel. The SS most of all wanted to implicate Canaris and Oster (who was dismissed from his Abwehr post on April 6), and hoped that this first group of jailed resisters would break in prison, that they would name names. But they didn't. Dr. Bonhoeffer wrote later that the news about his son, daughter, and son-in-law being arrested "didn't hit us unprepared, but given what one knew about the treatment of political prisoners it was a hard blow."[64]

The Nazi authorities had strict rules about who was permitted to send letters to or receive letters from prisoners and how often. Dietrich and Hans were allowed to write to their families only once every ten days during their initial "interrogation period." Karl-Friedrich Bonhoeffer didn't learn until late April that he could write to his youngest brother, but then he quickly forwarded a reassuring message, wanting to "send a signal that someone is thinking of you in your isolation.... Keep up your good spirits."[65] That injunction of course applied to the whole family. Prisons evoked dread and, in many quarters, shame, but the Bonhoeffers faced the difficulties with characteristic openness. And the Dohnanyis' home in Sakrow became a refuge where Christine, once she was released, managed to take care of an ever-growing number of family members.

On April 23, which was Good Friday, Hans wrote to Dietrich from his prison cell on Lehrterstrasse—not knowing, of course, whether the letter would be delivered. (To do so, he surrendered his right to send Easter letters to his children or parents-in-law.) His message was one of soul-searing regret: "That I am responsible for you, Christel, the children, and the parents having to bear this pain, that my beloved wife and you are robbed of freedom—you won't believe how this depresses me.... If I knew that you all—and you personally—don't think of me with reproaches, a weight would be lifted from my soul."[66]

Dietrich wrote back as soon as he could, similarly ignorant of whether his letter would reach Hans, avowing that "there is not a grain of reproach or bitterness in me regarding what has happened to you and me. Such things come from God, and only Him. And I know that you and Christel are at one with me, that before Him there is only submission, endurance, patience—and gratitude."[67]

On April 25, Easter Sunday, Christine was still in jail (she was released a week later), but she sent her children a long letter:

> My beloved children,
> ...Father is completely alone and so I always write to him and have asked him to write to you...my thoughts are always with you, and in addition I have time, time like never before in my life, to be alone with my thoughts....I read a lot [and] I also go for walks, always nicely back and forth in the cell by the open window. I eat from a nice white enameled bowl such as I have never had at home....Everything is always immediately at hand, for it lies either on the table or in the suitcase. I should like to introduce this at home. And in general one sees how good it is when one has few needs. Remember that. Not for the jail but for life....
>
> Now I want to tell you one more thing. Don't carry any hate in your heart against the power that has done this to us. Don't fill your young souls with bitterness; that has its revenge and takes from you the most beautiful thing there is, trust....
>
> Believe me, when one has experienced this, then one knows that it is after all only a really small and meager part of the human being that one can put in jail. I embrace all of you.[68]

Trust was still the family treasure. In a letter read by Nazi censors she would not have mentioned that her children—indeed all thinking people—lived in a world where trust had so often been easily and fatally betrayed.

It was not only that the lives of the Bonhoeffers, Dohnanyis, and others were so shockingly disrupted by these arrests. The British historian Sir John Wheeler-Bennett understood the political consequences:

> At one stroke, the [anti-Hitler] conspiracy [was] deprived of many of its most valuable treasures: the high integrity of Dietrich Bonhoeffer, the noble character and intellectual ability of Hans von Dohnanyi, the tireless courage and indomitable energy of Joseph Müller and the fearless ingenuity of Hans Oster. It was the end of the original conspiracy against Hitler.... Something departed with them; something intangible; something, it must be confessed, that was never really replaced, even by the fanatical zeal of Claus von Stauffenberg.[69]

V

DIETRICH BONHOEFFER WAS held at the Tegel prison in Berlin for eighteen months, at first in solitary confinement and then—thanks partly to his mother's intervention with her cousin General Paul von Hase—in somewhat less squalid quarters. (Tegel, an interrogation prison for military men, was a filthy, brutal, ugly place, but in his communications with his family Dietrich did not mention jail conditions, any more than his sister did during her weeks behind bars, or Hans von Dohnanyi.)

Our knowledge of what happened to Dietrich and Hans in the last two years of their lives remains scant, despite letters and testimonies. How did they withstand the horrors? How did they cope? None of it was easy, but they managed to keep in touch with their families through censored letters, coded messages, and visits, and the Bonhoeffers regularly brought the prisoners food, clean clothes, books, and whatever cheerful items they could. Hans and Dietrich also managed to learn about the ongoing conspiracy, and they knew enough about each other's situation to be able to coordinate their legal strategies.

For the first several months, in sessions of unremitting harsh interrogation, though without physical torture, Manfred Roeder would press hard on the reasons why Dietrich had obtained *u.k.* status and thus been exempted from an army call-up (was he trying to evade military service?—that was a crime), on his allegedly subversive acts (in Operation 7), on the reasons for his many trips outside Germany (was he trying to contact the enemy?) and from Pomerania to Berlin (had the Gestapo not banned him from the capital?). Dietrich would confess ignorance of the larger settings into which Roeder kept trying to place him, volunteering as little information as possible. Mercifully his many brave and risky actions against the Nazis in the long battle over the churches were of no interest to the prosecutor, who stuck to details about his Abwehr work and his exemption from military obligations. Every day Dietrich made every effort to maintain his energy for the nightmare sessions; from the start he worked to keep up his physical health and spiritual vigor by following a strict daily regimen—rising before dawn, reading and memorizing Scripture, meditating, exercising.

He was at first profoundly depressed not only by the callous, foulmouthed guards, the dirt and sweltering heat, and the bleak efficiency with which the prison isolated its inmates, but by his own grim assessment of the mistakes he might have made, and by his "separation from people, from work, from the past, from the future, from honor, from God...fading of memories...passing time—killing time...smoking and the emptiness of time," as he put it in a note to himself in May.[70] The worse it got, the less he wrote of his despair in the few letters he was allowed to send to family and friends.* In another note to himself later in 1943 he mentioned (only this once)

---

*Bonhoeffer had already lost many colleagues and friends in the war. His years in Pomerania had been filled with heartbreaking news not only of arrests, military drafts, and untold privations of his students and their families, but of battlefield deaths. Before he got to Tegel he had already written condolence letters to the families of twenty-five of his seminary students. See Bethge, *Dietrich Bonhoeffer*, p. 705; *Dietrich Bonhoeffer Werke*, Vol. 16, pp. 228–233 and passim.

"suicide, not out of a sense of guilt, but because I am practically dead already." But he needed no reminder that acedia was a cardinal sin and a "temptation...of which Luther so gravely warned," in which "a person disintegrates internally."[71]

Slowly he rediscovered truths he already knew: that preparing a strategy for his interrogations and focusing on clearing his name at an early trial gave him hope; that concentrating on the full meaning of the here and now, living fully in the moment—humanizing the execrable prison routines, cheering up his fellow inmates, getting to know the guards (several of whom showed themselves humane and sympathetic)—restored his inner equilibrium and gave him some kind of peace. Not to mention the daily reading of the Psalter and the prayers and hymns he shared with his fellow prisoners. "He was always so interesting and good-humored," wrote an Italian officer who was imprisoned with him. "He was the best and most gifted man I have ever met."[72]

For Hans incarceration was the beginning of unspeakable suffering; everything he had abhorred about the regime for ten dreadful years he now had to experience for himself—the Nazis' boundless criminality, their contempt for even basic decency, and their sadistic determination to destroy a person by threats and humiliation before actual extinction. And though like Dietrich he was spared physical torture, they both knew there was no immunity from it. Once Christine was released on April 30, she could give much-needed moral and practical support to him and to her brother, but he was in great danger, he was also ill, and he was alone—without Christine, with whom, as he so often recalled, he had hitherto shared all suffering and joy.

The family had expected that the worst of Nazi interrogative pressure would come down on Hans, and it did; accepting this had been part of the agreed-on strategy. But at least Christine could let him know that Admiral Canaris and other officers were doing what they could to help him and to thwart Roeder. So Hans like Dietrich focused on his recourse to the law, however corrupted, both men wanting the earliest possible chance to convince a judge of their innocence of the baseless charges about currency violations.

Over the summer of 1943 they each learned something of the further Allied successes in North Africa and the Allied landings in Sicily, so they could also hope simply to survive until Germany's defeat or until a putsch against Hitler succeeded—the operation for which Hans had done so much to prepare. In July, when Italy's Grand Council of Fascism deposed Mussolini and appointed General Pietro Badoglio as prime minister, it was for Hitler not only the loss of his first ally but an ominous warning. His health shaken, he alternated ever more between fantasy and fury; he was dissuaded from improvising a raid on Rome to take the new Italian authorities prisoner (and perhaps also those in the Vatican). The calamitous month ended with Hamburg suffering the worst air raid yet in the war, with a firestorm in which 30,000 citizens perished. Hitler was characteristically unmoved, though enraged at Göring and his Luftwaffe for allowing this to happen.

There was no letup that summer in Roeder's brutal interrogations about Operation 7—he was deliberately harsher and uglier with Hans than with Dietrich—but Hans outmaneuvered him, leading him into a bog of confusing technical details about currency transfers, all the while enduring streams of abuse, reminders of his Jewish descent, and threats of renewed imprisonment of his wife. Roeder kept hammering away at Dietrich's Abwehr activities and his travels abroad; he got nowhere with Hans on that front either.

Thanks in large part to steps taken by Hans's associates on the outside, along with his own carefully worded complaints about the conduct of the investigations, which he composed in his cell and sent to officials of the War Court, by midsummer Field Marshal Keitel conceded that the high-treason charges against both men should be dropped. And in the autumn both Dietrich and Hans were finally shown their indictments—though not the supporting evidence—on lesser but vexing charges about currency violations and a new Nazi high crime punishable by death: *Wehrkraftzersetzung*, variously translated as "sedition and defeatism" or "subversion of the war effort." Insinuations about corruption were appended.

They remained steadfast and gave no names—ever. Yet there was the desolation of being utterly at the mercy of their jailers, the deranging uncertainty of their situation. For Hans there was the wrenching pain of the almost unendurable separation from Christine, whom he most needed, most missed, most loved, and his anguish about Dietrich, for whom he felt responsible and whom he loved. He brooded on why he had thought he had the right to put the family in jeopardy, to sacrifice everything that was good in the private realm so as to combat evil in the public realm. And there was the ever-present fear: Would he, would the others, withstand torture?

Of these inner ordeals we have some record: there are Dietrich's famous letters from Tegel, so amazingly serene and uncomplaining on first reading, perhaps, but offering profound testimony to the spiritual travail of incarceration; and Hans, too, wrote to his wife and children from the prison on Lehrterstrasse and later from the concentration camp at Sachsenhausen. Indeed, the letters to and from Christine and the family were essential to his inner survival. His wife would rebuke him for his tormenting self-reproaches and lovingly do her best to restore his self-confidence and courage; without her solicitude he might have faltered. And there were secret messages to and from both men composed with astounding ingenuity in codes they had agreed upon earlier or invented in despair. Parcels of food and clothing also carried messages; the help these men received from outside was literally lifesaving.

Hans was in physical torment, too, for his intensely painful and debilitating phlebitis was worsening. But despite everything, despite confinement in a sweltering cell with barely a glimpse of the outside, his inventive fortitude gave him some relief: it was in prison that he taught himself to draw and paint; it was in prison that he drew his touching portraits of Christine, drew a lovely nosegay of flowers to give her for her birthday, and caught in a sketch the mad, twisted visage of Roeder, that mini-Freisler (see illustrations on page 89). Hans increasingly turned to the Bible; his earlier and perhaps unarticulated faith became more conscious, and it fortified him in moments of despair. He rejoiced in every ray of sun and in every birdsong that came his way. Somehow he preserved his strength, and despite everything he kept outsmarting Roeder.

In November 1943, heavy Allied air raids over Berlin reached Lehrterstrasse and an incendiary bomb hit Hans's cell; he suffered a brain embolism, with frightening effects, including speech impairment. His captors had no choice but to cede to demands that he be transferred to the Charité hospital, where he was put under the care of Professor Sauerbruch, and where his father-in-law's influence could be exerted more effectively than in the horror stations of the Gestapo. At the Charité Sauerbruch allowed Christine to see Hans every day, as well as visits from some of his closest friends and allies in the anti-Hitler conspiracy, among them Justus Delbrück and Justus Perels, who brought him up to date on their plans.

Sauerbruch repeatedly foiled Roeder's and the Gestapo's efforts to recapture Hans, but on January 21, 1944, in Sauerbruch's absence, a Wehrmacht doctor and two SS men appeared at his bedside, rearrested him, and took him away to a military hospital in Berlin-Buch. (Buch, a northeasterly suburb, was on the far side of bombed Berlin from the Dohnanyi home in Sakrow, to the west; it became harder for Christine to visit, when she was permitted.) At the same time, however, Roeder was removed from the Dohnanyi and Bonhoeffer cases. A number of factors contributed to this fortunate turn of events, including some instigated by Hans's allies in the Abwehr, but the final blow was that Roeder abusively insulted an Abwehr unit, whose commanding officer was outraged and ordered that Roeder be slapped in the face to make sure he understood.[73]

Dietrich had learned about Hans's embolism and hospitalization from his parents, and the news was terrible in more ways than one: not only was his brother-in-law dangerously ill but Dietrich's trial, repeatedly scheduled and postponed, would be put off yet again until Hans was well enough to be tried at the same time. The up-and-down uncertainty of the internment of both men continued. And the interrogations did, too—now conducted by the only slightly less brutish Walter Huppenkothen, a Rhenish lawyer who had been an SS officer since 1935, and F. X. Sonderegger from the Gestapo. These were men who believed that verbal threats and abusive language were more effective than physical torture. In normal times, Hans may have appeared as aloof, even cold; but when he was moved he would show his true feelings. In the torment of being powerless against these brutes, in the loneliness and fear of prison, the compassion he had so often shown for others may well have overwhelmed him. Wardens sympathetic to him reported that they often heard him sobbing in his cell after his interrogations.[74]

Dietrich used the solitude of his cell as he had used the solitude at Ettal to study ever more deeply the fundamental texts that he regarded as central; letters to his parents were filled with requests for books—from Plotinus to Dilthey to Kierkegaard to Thomas à Kempis (in Latin) to Ortega y Gasset. The nightmare Tegel life was changing and deepening him.

In April 1944, he noted in a letter to his parents how different the jail experience felt to him after a year of it. He was working to grasp the inner sense of it, and to use it for building strength and hope: "Things that we have worked out for ourselves, consciously or unconsciously, will never be forgotten, since they have changed from being powerful experiences to taking definite shape as clear insights, purposes, and plans, and as such will keep their meaning for our future life."[75] He started to write more often to Bethge, the one friend with whom he could share the theological aspects of his inner thoughts.

"What keeps gnawing at me is the question, what is Christianity, or who is Christ actually for us today?"[76] Dietrich's willingness to persist with this bold fundamental question is central to the value of his extraordinary prison letters. And the informal conversational tone he used with Bethge invites any reader to join in what was for him an ongoing quest to discover what life was really about, what life *should* be about. Given his experiences during the previous decade of quasi peace and outright war, it was no wonder that this lively, principled, warmhearted man, now thrust behind bars, was continuing to address basic issues from the ground up—freedom, coercion, trust, community, church, penitence, courage, free will, submission, resistance, death. And it is no surprise that having witnessed the capitulation of German churches to Nazi demands he wanted to think about religious faith apart from its institutionalized presence in society. The very dramatic setting in which Bonhoeffer initiated this conversation—from behind prison walls, and at the mercy of a foul, corrupt, evil regime—gives it still greater moral power.

What mattered most to him was the inner life of faith, which for him was not at all the life of someone trying to be pious or merely treasuring piety's outward forms; it was about "living unreservedly in life's duties, problems, successes and failures, experiences and perplexities." That, he believed, was how a true life of faith, a true Christian commitment, had to begin, by throwing oneself fully into the miseries and joys, the difficulties and terrors of daily life. "In so doing we throw ourselves completely into the arms of God, taking seriously not our own sufferings but those of God in the world.... How can success make us arrogant or failure lead us astray when we share in God's sufferings through a life of this kind?"[77]

The most controversial aspect of his letters to Bethge was (and still is) Bonhoeffer's interest in using them to explore what he called "religionless Christianity." He used the word "religion" almost pejoratively, referring to the outer forms of established faith practices; he thought that most of Christianity's encrusted habits and structures that had been revered for centuries might, even should, be jettisoned. Then one could ask, in a genuinely neutral and active way: Who is Jesus Christ for us now? What is the meaning of Christianity in our post-Enlightenment, rational, "grown-up" modern world [*Mündigkeit*] of people who believe they can manage important life issues without recourse to "Working hypothesis: God"? Did Christ or Christianity mean anything to them? What should it mean?

For a working pastor or theologian, these questions come together when thinking about baptism, the sign and signal of membership in a church. What value does baptism convey? Bonhoeffer had this question in mind in May 1944 especially because Eberhard's baby son, Dietrich Bethge, was about to be baptized. (Bethge had married one of Dietrich's nieces, Renate, daughter of Ursula and Rüdiger Schleicher.) "How I would have loved to baptize your little boy!" he wrote to them. "My wish for you is that you will look back on this day of baptism especially happily, and that it helps you fill this brief time together [during Eberhard's leave from his Wehrmacht unit in

Italy] with a substantial meaning that will last even through times of separation. Some memories torment, and some strengthen us. This day will be one that gives strength."[78]

He sent them a little homily he had prepared for the day—another magnificent text in which he unflinchingly acknowledged the force of destruction in war-torn Germany (which "tramples on our outward happiness") but also meditated on where the modern world was headed, and affirmed the soothing strengths of family, home, and music. The paragraphs are radiant with the imprisoned godfather's kindness and wisdom. And the endangered Dietrich did not want the meaning of his and Hans's experience to be lost:

> More clearly than in other ages, we realize that the world is in God's wrathful and merciful hands....It will be the task of our generation, not to seek "great things," but to save and preserve our souls out of the chaos....We learned too late that it not thought [considering all the options of an action in advance] but readiness to take responsibility that is the mainspring of action. Your generation will relate thought and action in a new way.[79]

In contrast to the months of imprisonment in 1943, when Hans and Dietrich, along with their families on the outside, did what they could to work for a speedy resolution at an early trial, by 1944 a survival strategy required delay; both men knew of the ongoing plan to topple the regime—Operation Valkyrie—that Hans had helped to set in motion. As Hans's health improved he began to think that in the short term only further illness could save him from the clutches of the Gestapo; he was safer in a hospital bed than a prison cell. In May he begged his wife to obtain, perhaps with her father's help, a means to infect him with diphtheria. The unflinching Christine did this, poisoning some of the food she brought for him on one of her authorized visits. The ghastly ploy worked, and Hans was taken to the army hospital for contagious diseases near Potsdam (which was much easier for Christine to reach). Huppenkothen continued his threatening interrogations there, but they gained him nothing.

In mid-July, after the Allied landings in Normandy, the authorities finally acknowledged to themselves that they lacked sufficient evidence to bring either Dohnanyi or Bonhoeffer to trial. The prosecutor who had taken over from Roeder advised Field Marshal Keitel that perhaps Hans should be interned in a sanitarium for the duration of the war and his trial postponed until after it.[80]

But everything changed irredeemably on July 20, 1944, when Hitler survived the now most celebrated effort to assassinate him. Bonhoeffer and Dohnanyi couldn't have known right away of the brutal, bloody aftermath of its failure—the murder in Berlin that very night at Wehrmacht headquarters in the Bendlerblock of the principal conspirators, who had been apprehended on the spot: generals Beck and Olbricht, the officers Claus von Stauffenberg and his adjutant Werner von Haeften. The Gestapo would not allow Christine to visit Hans, so she could not give him this news, but he would have intuited the rage that would be consuming the Nazi chieftains once they realized the extent of the opposition to them. Oster was arrested the next day, Canaris two days later.

A special commission was quickly established under Himmler's deputy, Ernst Kaltenbrunner, to hunt down every last accomplice or suspect in the plot. Over the next weeks, Kaltenbrunner and hundreds of frantic agents arrested many active resisters, including the young diplomat Hans-Bernd von Haeften (Werner's brother), Erwin Planck (Max Planck's son), and Paula Bonhoeffer's cousin General von Hase. The show "trials" for these "suspects" were conducted at the Peoples' Court by the ferociously nasty, red-robed Judge Freisler, his face contorted "in extremes of hatred and derision" as he screamed and hurled insults at the defendants.[81] (There were moments of great courage, though, as when Haeften calmly replied to Freisler's question about his motives, "Hitler was Evil's great perpetrator."[82]) The campaign continued for months; probably six thousand people were rounded up, tried, and most of them killed. Among those executed were General von Hase, Haeften, Moltke, Erwin Planck, Justus Perels, and Wilhelm Leuschner.

On August 22 Sonderegger ordered Hans's removal to the sick bay of the Sachsenhausen concentration camp, some thirty miles north of Berlin. And there Hans, still suffering from lingering diphtheria, which gave him peripheral paralysis in his feet and legs, heroically learned to feign that condition even after its physical disappearance. During those late-summer weeks, with no apparent change in their routine incarcerations (except that Hans was put in quarantine), Dietrich and Hans and their families could hope that they were at least safe from being implicated in the July 20 plot; their interrogators had no evidence leading in that direction.

But on September 22 the Gestapo found some of the documents that Hans had so assiduously collected and then stored in the Wehrmacht safe in Zossen; their secret location had been betrayed by an Abwehr chauffeur, disconsolate over the suicide of his boss, an Abwehr officer. Now Hans's persecutors comprehended his role in virtually every attempt that had been made since 1938 to overthrow the regime, found evidence of his carefully assembled networks and his close contacts with anti-Hitler activists from General Beck to the ex-Socialist leaders, and learned of the conspirators' overtures via the Vatican to Great Britain. On October 5 Huppenkothen stormed into Hans's sickroom and threw on his bed some photocopies of the Zossen documents: "Here we have what we have been seeking for two years!"*

In 1945–1946 some people faulted Dohnanyi for having allowed the documents to be preserved, since the Nazis' discovery of them led to the deaths of so many people. But in fact, immediately after his arrest and consistently thereafter when he could get the message through to his confederates via Christine, he had insisted that the papers be moved from Zossen and jettisoned. And this had indeed been done for a great many of them, including the "Chronicle of Shame" and materials relating to the years 1933–1937. It was General Beck who had countermanded his order about the later years because, Beck thought, the documents would be essential, once Nazi rule was at an end, in persuading Germans of the regime's criminality. To this line of reasoning Dohnanyi's response from his hospital bed had been, as his wife reported, "'This has always been Beck's argument, and a case can indeed be made for it. He should do what he thinks is right, but for God's sake he should see to it that nothing happens [to anyone as a result]. I owe that to the people over there' (by which he meant the Vatican and England)."[83] He knew that key aspects of the resistance work depended on a host of people, including diplomats and churchmen of other countries to whom the conspirators had moral obligations.

Some of the Zossen papers were shown to Hitler, who did indeed

---

*Christine wrote three brief statements about the fate of her husband and of the Zossen files from which we have drawn this account: a brief, undated one; the second in reply to inaccurate information that a German general gave the Allied authorities on July 20, 1945; and the third for American lawyers at the Nuremberg trials who wanted more complete information on the conspiracy. All three can be found in the appendix to Bethge, *Dietrich Bonhoeffer*, pp. 935–941. See also Smid, *Hans von Dohnanyi, Christine Bonhoeffer*, p. 433.

now recognize the full extent of the plots against his regime, and again he flew into a rage, at once deranged and determined. Countermanding earlier instructions for instant deaths, he now wanted his targets to be arrested, interrogated harshly—that is, tortured—put on trial, and disposed of with maximum humiliation. His fury knew no bounds: he had probably always distrusted all these superior men and minds, all these aristocrats with grand names and manners, and now he wanted them disgraced, strangled, dead.

On October 8, Dietrich Bonhoeffer and Josef Müller were moved from the military jail at Tegel to the prison cellar at Gestapo headquarters in Berlin on Prinz-Albrecht-Straße, known for years as an ultimate place of terror, where in 1933 thousands of Socialists and Communists had been thrown into "protective custody" and tortured. Oster, Canaris, Schlabrendorff, and others arrested after July 20 were among the other inmates who had already suffered for months in this fiendish place. Klaus Bonhoeffer, Rüdiger Schleicher, and Bethge were now also arrested and sent to the Lehrterstrasse prison, where Klaus was tortured. In these two prisons, and in other places of incarceration, was a German elite, together at last—powerless and destined to die.

Dietrich Bonhoeffer's interrogations were "frankly repulsive," he told Schlabrendorff, who was himself severely tortured, and they continued to focus almost entirely on Dietrich's trips abroad. By now he was adept at retelling limited truths so as to give his questioners no new information, or so he hoped.

Throughout the grim winter that followed, Christine did her best to look after her parents, who spent most of their nights in Sakrow, as did, after Schleicher's arrest in October, his wife and daughters. (Earlier, in February 1944, Christine and her mother had been family midwives when Renate Schleicher Bethge gave birth to her son Dietrich in Sakrow.) The Dohnanyis' home was a lifesaving refuge for the Bonhoeffers, Schleichers, and others who spent the nights there, but maintaining the household was very difficult for Christine, who had her own children to attend to, not to mention the absent Hans, and it became harder as food supplies dwindled; still, the family sent food to Hans and Dietrich whenever they could.[84]

February was the start of the long spring nightmare. Dohnanyi, his hands and legs still paralyzed, was brought on a stretcher from Sachsenhausen to the notorious Gestapo cellar on February 1. In the confusion caused by an air-raid alarm soon after, Dietrich miraculously managed to get to Hans's cell and have a brief clandestine conversation with him.

On February 2, the diabolical Judge Freisler sentenced Klaus Bonhoeffer and Rüdiger Schleicher to death. On February 3, Berlin endured its heaviest daytime bombardment yet (relentless Allied bombing continued until mid-April); the Peoples' Court was in flames and the Central Security Office took a direct hit (though this did not affect the prisoners in the cellar). Karl and Paula Bonhoeffer were unable, hard as they tried, to make their way across the rubble to deliver a birthday letter and package to Dietrich. Rüdiger Schleicher's brother Rolf (a doctor), who had rushed home from the eastern front to be present at Rüdiger's trial and arrived a day late, was trying to get to the Peoples' Court when he was asked to help with a bloodied, possibly dead body in the courtyard there: he could see that the person was indeed dead. It was Freisler; the corpse was clutching papers about Schlabrendorff in one hand.[85] A few days later the Bonhoeffers got through to Prinz-Albrecht-Straße. Their letter was the last communication from parents to son; Dietrich had been taken from Berlin, no one knew to where.

Weeks later, Hans wrote Christine an intensely loving and also daringly precise letter—composed over several days—about how they should conduct themselves in the next weeks. On a dozen little circles of cardboard (the cut-off bottoms of paper cups) covered with very small handwriting, he made their resolute intentions clear: "[The prison commandant] has a soft spot for his prisoners and is angling for an anchor to the future...gaining time is the only solution. I must see to it that I become unable to be interrogated. It would be best if I could get a respectable *dysentery* [*Ruhr*]...but I am not afraid of *any* illness."[86] With her father's help Christine complied. But the interrogations continued. Sonderegger told him they knew everything about the July 20 plot already and did not need him to name names; they only wanted his general impressions of the conspiracy, in return for which they would release him. He refused to say anything. Asked for his motives in opposing National Socialism, he replied, "arbitrariness in matters of law, and National Socialist procedures in Jewish and church questions."[87] His guards were ordered to abandon him, essentially leaving him unable to move, lying sick and alone in his soiled bed for three weeks. And still, nothing broke him.

On March 8 the utterly exhausted Hans, who was still being interrogated, asked his wife to infect him again, "as far as I'm concerned with cholera or typhoid."[88] On March 19 he was moved to a prison hospital in Berlin—again with the hidden help of his father-in-law. And there a police doctor appeared, Albrecht Tietze, a humane (and anti-Nazi) physician who restored some decency to his care and, perhaps most important, befriended him. Tietze treasured his conversations with Hans, whose insights and moral strength he admired; he sensed that Hans was telling him important things—a final legacy, as it were (*Vermächtnis*)—and he conveyed to Christine the essence of them.

Dohnanyi told Tietze that he had realized from the very beginning that the regime was moving toward war and disaster and that only a revolution could stop it, but "the obtuseness and cowardice of people of property and influence, and the stupidity of most officers, frustrated all efforts." Only intrepid workers and disciplined Socialists of the sort Dohnanyi met in Sachsenhausen had it in them to be effective resisters, he thought. He told Tietze over and over again about the men he had found in prison whose value he had recognized at once. Did it have to be that it was only in a concentration camp, when it was too late, that he encountered these "unblemished idealists, hardened by suffering," who would have given the resistance its ultimate promise for the future?[89]

The end was coming in different forms. Dietrich rejected a serious attempt at escape, as did Hans, for whom Tietze made detailed, risky arrangements. We may assume that as much as they wanted to break free, they feared the mortal consequences for their families.

Hans's will to survive was as strong as ever, crippled though he was by illness real or feigned. He even thought about whether he could speak with Himmler, somehow guessing that this terrible man, bereft of any sense of justice or humanity, caring only about his own survival, might possibly be of aid. He wasn't wrong: he could not have known, but perhaps he sensed, that Himmler was conniving to use Hans's Swedish contacts for his own benefit.* But Dietrich and he, and their stalwart associates, hoped above all that they could stay alive until the day of Germany's final defeat.

It was not to be. On April 5, at a noon meeting, Hitler issued specific instructions to execute the Canaris group. Dr. Tietze was told to transfer Dohnanyi back to the medical station in Sachsenhausen; after giving Christine a signal so that she could see her husband one

---

*That very month, in conversations with Count Bernadotte of Sweden, who was representing the Allies, Himmler was scheming to bring about Germany's negotiated surrender and thus to save his own skin, too, even promising the release of "female Jews from Ravensbrück." See Ian Kershaw, *The End: The Defiance and Destruction of Hitler's Germany, 1944–1945* (Penguin, 2011), pp. 336–337.

last time that evening, he sedated Hans very heavily. The next day, the SS court-martial took place, with Huppenkothen as the prosecutor. Hans was mercifully still drugged and only intermittently conscious, so thus was spared the last offense: that of having to participate in this travesty of justice with its foreordained "verdict" of high treason, punishable by death. The next morning he was carried on a stretcher to the place of his execution and hanged.*

The Nazis had wreaked their vengeance. After seeing the Zossen documents, the Gestapo agents had boasted that Dohnanyi was "the spiritual head of the conspiracy" to eliminate Hitler.[90]

Buchenwald was the concentration camp built by the Nazis in the "beech woods" near the cradle of German idealism—the town of Weimar. And it was Buchenwald to which Dietrich and other Gestapo prisoners had been taken. By April 1, Easter Sunday, Allied forces were quite close to it, having fought their way across the Rhine and into Germany during the previous month. The camp guards, hearing the rumble of American cannon, wondered what the high command wanted them to do with their prisoners, let alone themselves. On April 3 in the middle of the night, some guards took away a group of prisoners in a big truck and drove them south in the direction of the slave-labor camp at Flossenbürg, then past it. The meandering, seemingly pointless trip went on for a few more days; several survivors of the macabre excursion remembered Bonhoeffer's calm, reassuring presence throughout—even when the truck broke down as it was returning them first to Schönberg and then Flossenbürg, even when they rightly feared the worst.

The Gestapo and SS had orders to obey and work to do, no matter

---

*The Nazis murdered millions of people without so much as a feint to "the law," but usually when it concerned fellow Germans they punctiliously followed it, preserving the judicial forms while violating their substance.

how close the enemy. Huppenkothen, together with his pregnant wife, arrived at the Flossenbürg camp on Sunday, April 8, in a convoy of cars carrying them and various other high officials along with documents, luggage, and extra gasoline; the group had fled Berlin and was heading south to escape into territory not yet in Allied hands. But first there were murders to attend to. An SS judge dispatched from Nuremberg dutifully made his way there by freight train and, for the last twelve miles, by bicycle. At the request of some of the prisoners Dietrich held a short Sunday service in the courtyard at Schönberg, his homily on a text from Isaiah: "With his wounds we are healed." At the summary court-martial held that night in Flossenbürg by the bicyclist judge, with Huppenkothen again the prosecutor, Bonhoeffer, Canaris, Oster, and several others were condemned to death; they were hanged there early the next morning. Dietrich was composed to the last.

VI

IN MAY 1945 Europe was in dark, uncertain chaos, its people anxious, ill fed, and, especially in Eastern Europe, in shock over the many millions of men and women who had lost their lives in the war, over the devastation of the landscape and the destruction of cities. Other Europeans could at least rejoice in the Allied victory that brought them liberation from the German scourge, but Germans faced defeat, and only a few of them saw it as a liberation. Most, living in a cloud of unknowing about missing kin, were benumbed and hungry. All that mattered was family and food.

The Bonhoeffers, Dohnanyis, Schleichers, and Delbrücks shared this horror. They were desperately holding on in the bombed-out ruins of Berlin, with most means of communication cut, with food as scarce as information, with new foreign masters in charge of their city, and with no idea where their husbands, brothers, and sons might be or what had happened to them. Frantically they went on searching.

Justus Delbrück was released from prison in late April—"I made it: I am back again!" he wrote to his wife on April 30[91]—but the Russians rearrested him, purportedly for only a few days to gain information about the anti-Hitler resistance. But he never made it home. He died of diphtheria in a former Nazi, now Soviet prison camp in October.

The Schleichers learned at the very end of May that Rüdiger, along with Klaus Bonhoeffer, Hans John, Justus Perels, and others, had been in a group of men taken at night from the Lehrterstrasse prison and shot to death just a hundred yards away, on the fairgrounds near the prison; these Gestapo murders occurred on April 23, when the Red Army had already reached the outskirts of Berlin. Klaus had written an Easter letter—essentially a farewell—to his children, which eventually they received. It concluded:

> The times of horror, of destruction, and of dying, in which you, dear children, are growing up, demonstrate the transitoriness of all earthly things, for all the glory of a human being is like the flower of the grass...we lead our lives aware of this....But here begins all the wisdom and piety that turns away from the transitory to the eternal....Do not remain in the twilight but rather struggle toward clarity...take for yourself possession of this world in which what matters most is what you in all honesty have experienced and acquired. Then your lives will be blessed and happy. Farewell! God keep you![92]

For Christine von Dohnanyi and her children the anguish went on longer. Until July, she had reason to hope that Hans might still be alive, and it was only in December 1945 that she felt certain enough of his fate to place a newspaper obituary: "We must now take it as a certainty," it read, that Hans von Dohnanyi met his death in April after "two years in the Sachsenhausen concentration camp. He gave his life in his faith in God and in the law and in great love for Germany. *'Blessed are the dead which die in the Lord from henceforth: Yea, saith the Spirit, that they may rest from their labors; and their works do follow them.'* Revelation 14:13"[93]

Karl-Friedrich Bonhoeffer, busy in Leipzig trying to reestablish his laboratory and uncertain whether the Russians would permit him to continue there, indeed uncertain that he would survive, wrote to his children (who had been evacuated from Berlin in mid-June), both to give them a report and to ask for family news. He had been in the capital in late March and had heard virtually nothing since. He told them about the ceaseless rounds that he and their aunts had made then to take news, food, and necessities to their uncles in jail:

> Those Berlin prisons! What did I know of them just a few years ago, and with what different eyes have I looked on them since. The Charlottenburg interrogation prison, where Aunt Christel was held...the Tegel military interrogation prison where Uncle Dietrich was interned...the Moabit military prison with Uncle Hans, the SS prison on Prinz-Albrecht-Strasse where Uncle Dietrich was kept behind bars in the cellar...and the Lehrter Strasse prison where they tortured Uncle Klaus and tormented Uncle Rüdiger....

And he asked after his parents: "Is everyone still alive? Did your grandparents manage all right through those difficult days?" Despairingly he inquired as to Dietrich's whereabouts.[94]

Dietrich's fate was unknown to them all until sometime after Martin Niemöller and Fabian von Schlabrendorff met—by sheer chance—in May. Schlabrendorff, whose trial had been aborted by the death of Roland Freisler, had been moved from the Gestapo prison in Berlin first to Sachsenhausen, then to the slave-labor camp at Flossenbürg, where he learned of the deaths of Bonhoeffer and Oster, Canaris and Olbricht; then he was moved to Dachau, where he soon found himself, along with Niemöller, who had been in Dachau for years, in a group of 142 prisoners whom SS guards marched south toward the Alps. The SS guards abandoned their prisoners in the

South Tyrol's forested mountains on May 4—and then evaporated. At some point in this macabre hike, Schlabrendorff told Niemöller the terrible news about Bonhoeffer's death, and once Niemöller reached a functioning telegraph office in Italy he sent a message (the connections to Berlin were broken and inoperable) to Visser 't Hooft in Geneva; the news then wended its way to the Leibholzes in Oxford and eventually to the parents and Maria in Berlin.

Karl and Paula Bonhoeffer, plagued by fleeting illness—in her case brought on by malnutrition as well as the pains of age—and grieving over the murders of two sons and two son-in-laws (a family fate perhaps unique in Germany then), nevertheless carried on with remarkable fortitude. Christine well expressed the unimaginable pain: in September she wrote to her and her husband's friend Otto John, another Lufthansa lawyer (whose brother Hans had been shot along with Klaus Bonhoeffer and Rüdiger Schleicher on April 23), "I believe it is better [schöner] to know for what one dies than not to know what exactly one is living for." To her mother she confessed she couldn't imagine that the family could ever be happy again, "and yet that is precisely what we owe the dead. I can't get it straight...."[95] She—like her brother Klaus in a farewell letter he had written to their parents at the end of March—recalled the shock of her brother Walter's death in 1918, and remembered that even after it the family contrived to have many convivial occasions together. Grief about the dead strengthened responsibility for the living, especially for the surviving half-orphaned children; the burdens of the moment required their constant care, and the will to survive was itself a moral command.

The Bonhoeffers and other survivors of the resistance faced pervasive calumny in defeated Germany. For many Germans, people like the Bonhoeffers who had plotted against Hitler or resisted the Nazi regime were traitors who had betrayed their country. Understandably, people were overwhelmed by their own personal tragedies and by the national catastrophe: the devastation was total, and the swelling stream of millions of Germans expelled from the east, from East Prussia or Silesia or the Sudetenland, intensified the suffering. "Who is to blame for this?" became the inevitable question. And it was easier to fault the Allies, the "betrayers of Yalta," than to acknowledge that the tribulations had been brought on by the Nazis or indeed by themselves. Many Germans had no time or heart to grieve or to feel responsible for the victims of war who were not German, and no time at all for those whose tragedies were related to their opposition to the Nazi regime.

The Bonhoeffer family was realistic in this ambiguous, compromised universe and continued courageously, though in November 1947 Dr. Bonhoeffer acknowledged to his Swiss colleague, the eminent psychiatrist Ludwig Binswanger, "The war and the Nazi years, with all their evil consequences for our family, did somewhat drain us [hat uns doch etwas zermürbt]."[96] More immediately, the paterfamilias had to worry about his own financial situation and that of his surviving family: the Soviet commanders (in whose occupation zone the Charité lay) refused to pay pensions for former Prussian civil servants, so Dr. Bonhoeffer asked to be put back on the list of active physicians there; he received some kind of research grant and served as consultant to two West Berlin hospitals; and he still had some private patients. Having suffered under one unjust regime, he was now suffering under another.[97]

The Bonhoeffers were helped both physically and psychologically by former colleagues and friends now living outside Germany, who could reach out to them in the postwar years. In September 1948, two months before his death, Karl Bonhoeffer wrote in his crisp, clear hand to Dr. Rudolf Stern, reminiscing about former Breslau colleagues and depicting Berlin's wretched condition during the Airlift:

Karl Bonhoeffer's letter of September 15, 1948,
to Dr. Rudolf Stern (Fritz's father).
Dr. Bonhoeffer died only weeks later.

"One has to recall over and over again that what millions had to endure under the Hitler regime was incomparably harder than what we must bear today. Still, Berlin is richly saddled with miseries and would be grateful for a little quiet."* But the Bonhoeffer spirit was uncommon in the festering horrors of 1945–1948, for many Germans had not rid themselves of Nazi poison.

Who had the moral authority to educate Germans in the truth, to recall the atrocities that every Bonhoeffer was conscious of? In 1947 Dr. Bonhoeffer wrote a withering, psychologically astute portrait of Germany under Hitler (published only after his death in 1949). In this medical-moral analysis, he raised a fundamental question that very few of his contemporaries did. As to the question whether Hitler was psychotic or schizophrenic, he believed the answer would require more evidence than was then available, but

more important for the judgment of the German people and the future is the question how was it possible that a regime that openly manifested inhuman brutality, violated the law [*Rechtsbruch*] in every way, intentionally exterminated valuable and for the future of Germany indispensable human capital [*Menschenmaterial*], and displayed corruption and immeasurable human arrogance [*Überheblichkeit*], how could such a regime maintain itself with the German people for twelve years and command millions of followers?†

---

*He added that the painting of Ursula and Christine, which "your parents gave us, has survived and hangs in my wife's room." Paula added a postscript: "Lieber 'Rudi Stern'! How often I heard your name from our children! . . . With what pleasure I think back to the good days of our children and their youth."

†"Führerpersönlichkeit und Massenwahn," in Zutt et al., *Karl Bonhoeffer*, p. 111 ff. In 1947, Dr. Bonhoeffer compared the medical consequences of the two world wars. Repeating his views about the "so-called exhaustion influences" endured in World War I, and "the

He partly answered his own question by referring to the Nazis' ceaseless propaganda, intimidation, and mass manipulation, and in many ways he echoed Dietrich's thoughts in "After Ten Years."

In 1945 the German Evangelical Church made several attempts to "explain" its position during the Nazi years, but in the end these amounted to mere pronouncements about atrocities, like the murder of Jews, that the regime had committed, the regime that, it quickly added, had persecuted or silenced the church itself.[98] It would seem that the Germans' spirit of "loyalty," their wartime will to fight to the end, to cling to their faith in the Führer, was transmuted after their nation's defeat into a kind of defiance, with resentment dominating the popular mood. And after all, Germany in 1945 didn't really exist—occupied as it was by the victorious Allied powers, partitioned by them into four different zones, and united primarily in self-pity and anguish.

Gert Leibholz in England understood the violent covert ambiguities of occupied Germany. He was torn between staying in England for a while and seeking a position in a German university, where he would have to work with ex-Nazi law professors who made a point of claiming they had purged themselves of their compromised past.

---

ability of the psyche to tolerate their effects" being "almost absolute," he contrasted this with experiences in World War II, noting that "there is a limit to the individual's psychic ability to endure [*Tragfähigkeit*] excessive bodily torment and humiliating procedures," notably the "inhuman and repulsive" torture that includes "brutal threats to imprison wife and children.... [These] apparently exceed psychic tolerance." He made no explicit mention of his family's experiences in either of these articles.

In July 1947 in a letter to a colleague, Dr. Bonhoeffer argued against death sentences for euthanasia murderers and for war criminals generally. He argued instead for life sentences of forced labor, and explained his abhorrence of executions as being related to his experience of the Gestapo killings of members of his family. See his "Vergleichende psychopathologische Erfahrungen aus den beiden Weltkriegen" and Gerrens, *Medizinisches Ethos und theologische Ethik*, pp. 57–63.

In 1947 he agreed to give some guest lectures at his old university of Göttingen, then accepted a full professorship there in 1951, and was one of the first lawyers to be nominated and appointed to West Germany's new Constitutional Court, where he served with distinction until retiring in 1971; he died in 1982. He wrote a fine appreciation of his brother-in-law and fellow lawyer Dohnanyi.[99]

Surviving resisters to the Nazi regime and surviving families of murdered resisters were often treated more badly and more dishonorably than surviving Nazi officials, many of whom managed quite well. No heed was taken of the resisters' earlier efforts or their families' present suffering, and unlike the executioners, they were usually denied their pensions, at least at first. And it took a full decade for West German officials to accord the "conspirators" of July 20 recognition as heroes rather than vilification as "traitors," when the Federal Republic's armed forces, the Bundeswehr, established in 1955, introduced an annual commemorative service on July 20 to honor them at the Bendlerblock. (An earlier event, organized by groups of survivors and descendants, took place on July 20, 1954.*) Only in the 1960s, after his mother's death in 1965, did Klaus von Dohnanyi succeed in having his father's and his uncle's death sentences legally annulled.

Consider, on the other hand, Manfred Roeder, the high-ranking Nazi prosecutor responsible for the deaths of Red Orchestra members and associates, and for arresting, then tormenting Dohnanyi and Bonhoeffer. In September 1945, Adolf Grimme, a Social Democrat (he had been Prussia's culture minister in the 1920s), sued Roeder for

---

*Ferdinand Schlingensiepen's unreliable biography of Bonhoeffer mistakenly asserts that "Adenauer, though he had been consistently opposed to Hitler, never attended these ceremonies" on July 20; *Dietrich Bonhoeffer 1906–1945*, p. xvii. As it happens, I (F.S.) saw Adenauer with my own eyes at the first commemoration at the Bendlerblock on July 20, 1954; he even spoke briefly at the occasion. The ceremony had an enduring effect on me.

having broken German law in prosecuting the Red Orchestra people on treason charges. It took the West German judicial system until 1951 to *dismiss* this case against the Nazi lawyer and to pronounce that treason had always been an abominable crime, one of which the July 20 conspirators were also guilty.[100]

Roeder, once cleared (and giving himself his full Nazi title as Judge General), published a small book on the Red Orchestra in which he maligned and mocked the resisters he had condemned, specified what harm "these Communists" had done, and declared that to understand their aims one only had to look at Germany's eastern zone or other satellite countries controlled by the Soviet Union. But his main point was not just to accuse them and heap praise on himself for prosecuting them but to warn the German public that every day "the web of the Red Orchestra is woven anew," that the Red conspiracy was a live danger.* (The US Army's Counter-Intelligence Corps had already recruited Roeder in 1949 as an informant about alleged Communist subversion in Germany.) The "cleared" Roeder became an active member of the Christian Democratic Union and deputy mayor of a small Hessian town, and in that dignified office died peacefully in 1971, unapologetic and unreconstructed to the end.

---

*Manfred Roeder, *Die Rote Kapelle: Europäische Spionage* (Hamburg: Hans Siep, 1952). A different Manfred Roeder, born in 1929, is well known in Germany as an anti-Semitic Holocaust-denying neo-Nazi whose political activities have earned him considerable prison time.

On the fate of the Nazi "judges" in the Dohnanyi and Bonhoeffer cases, see Josef Ackermann, *Dietrich Bonhoeffer—Freiheit hat offene Augen: Eine Biographie* (Gütersloh: Gütersloher Verlagshaus, 2005), pp. 248–259. Ackermann's is a competent study, with some errors, including his conflating Roeder the tormentor of Bonhoeffer and Dohnanyi with the other, younger Roeder. On the question of German postwar trials, see also *NS-Prozesse und deutsche Öffentlichkeit: Besatzungszeit, frühe Bundesrepublik und DDR*, ed. Jörg Osterloh and Clemens Vollnhals (Göttingen: Vandenhoeck & Ruprecht, 2011), p. 60.

The West German public and West German justice seemed almost eager to exonerate Nazi officials and to vilify or traduce the resisters. Walter Huppenkothen, to take another example, was brought before West German courts three times on charges of complicity in the trials and murders of Dohnanyi in Sachsenhausen and of Canaris, Oster, Bonhoeffer, and the others in Flossenbürg. (Like Roeder, Huppenkothen also did postwar work for the Americans; these Nazi villains serving as clandestine servants of the occupying power were known in the Counter-Intelligence Corps under the code names of, respectively, Othello and Fidelio.) The prosecutors argued that those trials had violated even Nazi laws. Huppenkothen's defense was that in prosecuting Dohnanyi and the others and then condemning them to death, he had been obeying lawful orders that came from Hitler and his circle (a frequent alibi). The courts ruled in Huppenkothen's favor, saying that only those who had given the orders were culpable. In 1956, the Bundesgerichtshof, West Germany's Supreme Court, upheld these acquittals.*

It was not until 2002, on what would have been Hans von Dohnanyi's hundredth birthday, that the then president of the Supreme Court, Günter Hirsch, at a ceremony honoring Dohnanyi's memory, declared that the 1956 decision in the Huppenkothen cases "must make one ashamed," and that it had had "devastating" consequences: "in the Federal Republic hardly any judges or prosecutors

---

*Germany's most distinguished legal scholar concludes his classic work on German law with this observation: "Silence was the precondition of a new beginning for the generation that had survived, and this was true of both victims and perpetrators.... [That silence] may also have come from an unconscious sentiment of gratitude and remorse to have escaped undeservedly from an inferno to which one had, actively or passively, contributed." Michael Stolleis, *Geschichte des öffentlichen Rechts in Deutschland, Vol. 3, Staats- und Verwaltungsrechtswissenschaft in Republik und Diktatur, 1914–1945* (Munich: C.H. Beck, 1999), p. 414.

involved in the thousands of judicial crimes [*Justizverbrechen*] of the Third Reich were convicted."[101] And it was only in 2003 that Yad Vashem registered Dohnanyi as a "righteous gentile." (There was a dignified ceremony at the Bonhoeffer house in Berlin with the then head of the oppositional Christian Democratic Union, Angela Merkel, and her husband in attendance.)

We might want to ask: Who were the more typical representatives of Germany after its defeat, Roeder and Huppenkothen, or the surviving members of the Bonhoeffer family?

Dietrich Bonhoeffer is often hailed as the brave pastor who was executed for his role in the plot to kill Hitler, but we have seen that that is not quite the case. The greatness of his achievement in the Nazi years came not so much from his involvement in the anti-Hitler operations as from his steadfast opposition to National Socialism within the German Evangelical Church, his valorous efforts to gain international recognition for the Confessing Church, and his lived commitment to a free church and a free country. After the war, many German pastors wanted to emphasize his church work and dissociate their fallen colleague from any tyrannicidal activity, of which they strongly disapproved; others were happy to do the opposite, emphasizing his participation in the anti-Hitler plots and averting their eyes from the sorry record of their churches' collusion with the dictator. It was convenient simply to transform Bonhoeffer into an icon of heroic German Protestantism; that one could call him a martyr made it even better.

Anglo-Saxon countries saw Bonhoeffer's heroic value somewhat more clearly—and sooner. There are many reasons for this, an obvious one being that Dietrich's twin sister and her husband, along with Franz Hildebrandt, Bishop George Bell, and others in England could arrange a memorial service for him in London (which the BBC broadcast) as early as July 1945. But there are doctrinal reasons, too. In his sermon at that service in London, Bishop Bell easily conjoined the dual aspects of Dietrich's heroism as representing "both the resistance of the believing soul, in the name of God, and also the moral and political revolt of the human conscience against injustice and cruelty." But doctrinaire Lutherans who insisted on a clear line separating church commitments from political ones did not seem to be able to do this, and their silence continued—even when, in 1998, a statue of Bonhoeffer was installed over the Great West Door of Westminster Abbey next to those of other sainted churchmen.

But a price was paid for this posthumous fame. The elevation of Bonhoeffer to iconic martyrdom occluded the larger, more significant German historical drama in which he played such an important part, and in which the man who decisively turned him from church opposition to state resistance is a major figure. In 1995, Eberhard Bethge noted the regrettable tendency among some modern historians "to play down Hans von Dohnanyi's role in the resistance movement."[102] Might Bethge himself, however unwittingly, have contributed to this "tendency"? Whoever is responsible, it is historically wrong and morally unjust to Dohnanyi, who at the very end of his life was haunted by having involved Dietrich in the anti-Hitler plots.

Inevitably—as is so common in history—the question remains: Is Bonhoeffer remembered correctly? Is the human decency he so well exemplified honored equally with his theological legacy? Is Dohnanyi's decency also honored, as well as his preservation, in an utterly corrupted state, of the highest standard of civic virtue? Both men's lives offer lasting moral instruction.

Though the world knows of Bonhoeffer in detail and hardly at all of Dohnanyi, they deserve to be remembered together. The Third Reich had no greater, more courageous, and more admirable enemies than they. Dohnanyi aptly summed up their work and spirit when he said they simply took "the path that a decent person inevitably takes." So few traveled that path—anywhere.

Appendix

THE LITERATURE BY and about Dietrich Bonhoeffer began to be published right after the war with volumes supervised by his friend, student, and legatee Eberhard Bethge. In 1946, Bethge arranged for the posthumous publication of poems Bonhoeffer had written in prison. A second edition, which also included three letters that Dietrich's brother Klaus had written to members of his family, appeared a year later. Bethge turned next to Dietrich's unfinished prewar book about ethics, which he saw into print in 1949. He had imagined that much would be made of *Ethics*, but it was greeted mostly with silence.

In the case of *Letters and Papers from Prison*, which came next, he made a reverse miscalculation: he aimed for a small book composed principally of letters that revealed Bonhoeffer's theological ideas as he was exploring them during his incarceration, but it turned out that readers, grateful as they were for this unusual, sometimes startling material, wanted to know more about the underlying human drama. That drama—about the Bonhoeffer family and the activities of the anti-Hitler resistance—dominated the background to the letters, as Bethge knew, but it hadn't been his purpose to go in that direction. John de Gruchy, a biographer of Bethge and the editor of the definitive English edition of *Letters and Papers from Prison*, explains: "Bethge undertook the task ... in order to share with a wider public [Bonhoeffer's] exciting new thoughts about the future of Christianity. ... The decision to publish these ['theological'] letters determined the original structure and content of the first edition ... and has generally influenced the way in which the volume has been received and understood."[103]

Over the next decades, Bethge and his editorial associates did tend in the other direction, though: he amplified *Letters and Papers from Prison* so that readers had more and better information about the Bonhoeffer family and about Dietrich's oppositional and then resistance work, though the book's fundamental structure did not change. In 1967, he saw yet another heavily corrected and reedited edition into print; one critic welcomed it as so far superior to the initial book that "all copies of previous editions should be gathered together and burned."[104] By then public understanding of Germany during the war years had deepened, and Bethge revised the book yet again; a fourth edition (published in English in 1971 and still the most widely available one in English) was twice the length of the original. Bethge explained: "The private element has been heightened. ... Nevertheless, the reader will find that he can encounter at greater depth an authentically attested piece of the history of our time," as well as being "part of the history of Christian devotion and theology."

Letters and Papers from Prison indeed has these attributes, but one may also observe that Franz Hildebrandt, who knew Dietrich's theological mind in the 1930s as well as anyone, declined to say much about it, since it was composed of material that he found unfinished and wanting; Karl Barth, too, was uneasy about its fragmentary nature.[105] And in truth, while these early volumes edited by Bethge leave one with admiration for Bonhoeffer's mind and heart, one may question the curious, ahistorical way that Bethge kept adjusting what he chose to publish from the luminous material that his friend had deeded to him. The excellent, now definitive edition of *Letters and Papers from Prison* (published in 2010, Volume 8 in the *Dietrich Bonhoeffer Works*) is *again* almost double the length of its 1971 forebear, a prodigious 774 pages of German and Anglophone erudition (the title page lists twelve laborers), and a tribute to scholarly devotion.

Martin E. Marty has written a small book considering the "biography" of *Letters and Papers from Prison* that doesn't much dwell on these transformations, which is perhaps a pity, for after all, the very purpose, body, and meaning of the book kept being altered. Still, Marty well depicts how Bonhoeffer's enigmatic, fragmentary, embryonic epistolary musings evoked strong responses, which he catalogs —from the postwar churches in East and West Germany, from liberation theology priests in Latin America, from Catholics and Protestants everywhere. Naturally, human nature being what it is, the various interpreters of Bonhoeffer used his book "to legitimize their own theological agendas," as one distinguished Bonhoeffer scholar has put it,[106] but Marty is charitable toward possible misreadings.

Bethge's initiative with *Letters and Papers from Prison* led to other Bonhoeffer texts being edited, corrected, and reedited by him or other scholars and translators, vetted by him and working in his shadow. Eventually almost everything Bonhoeffer wrote, or wrote down, was collected in seventeen volumes of *Dietrich Bonhoeffer Werke* or, in English, sixteen volumes of *Dietrich Bonhoeffer Works*. Of value to those who want or need the whole dossier, the enterprise has the weakness of all such unwieldy monuments: its close-up attention to every detail, its assiduous editorial apparatus, repeatedly adjusted and updated, seem to us to ascribe to Bonhoeffer more significance than may be appropriate, the implicit presumption being that everything he did was important, everything he wrote worthy of preservation. Bonhoeffer himself never claimed this.

Another basic source for Bonhoeffer scholars is Bethge's massive biography of his friend, first published in 1967 and after eight revised and expanded editions coming in at more than a thousand pages. One should respect this remarkable book but also remember that Bethge himself acknowledged his lack of training as a historian or biographer, having embarked on his immense effort out of affectionate loyalty and for what he said were principally theological reasons. His diligent exposition of Bonhoeffer's work and life is trustworthy, but a reader can lose track of the narrative, given the somewhat wooden arrangement of blocks of background information about theological or ecclesiastical people, issues, and events that are interspersed with nuggets of quotidian detail. Also, understandably if ironically, since this weakness is in part due to Bethge having been almost too close to Bonhoeffer and his relatives, he somehow did not keep them in sharp focus or recognize fully the centrality of Dietrich's brother-in-law. And since Bethge wrote in German for German readers, many of whom would be familiar with the repellent details of German conduct between 1933 and 1945, he mostly just set down facts; his sound appraisal of the political pressures under which the Bonhoeffers lived and worked is muted, and delivered rather monotonously. Still, this now gigantic book has genuine moral force.

Bethge was scrupulous, but his biography was marked by strange lapses, inconsistencies, and errors, most of which were corrected and recorrected in the oft-revised editions. Though subsequent Bonhoeffer scholars have complemented and filled out Bethge's interpretation, they haven't much challenged it: after half a century one would welcome a new perspective on the subject by someone coming to the subject afresh, but this doesn't seem to happen. Two recent biographies by Ferdinand Schlingensiepen and Eric Metaxas, their boasted "new documentation" notwithstanding, show a pronounced dependence on Bethge not only because the authors acknowledge it as a badge of honor but because their accounts follow Bethge's narrative so closely and in so many ways. This is very obvious in the glib Metaxas book, though the author strikes a lively new tone; he goes in a strange new theological direction, however, and betrays throughout a quite amazing ignorance of the German language, German history, and German theology.* His effort to capture Bonhoeffer for the cause of fundamentalist evangelicalism blurs the historical portrait, as do new distortions, omissions, and anachronisms.

Both Dietrich Bonhoeffer and Hans von Dohnanyi deserve further studies of the highest exactitude, as does the history of resistance and collaboration in Germany during Hitler's reign.

BOOKS BY DIETRICH BONHOEFFER

The Cost of Discipleship. Translated by R. H, Fuller. London: SCM Press, 1955. Originally published as *Nachfolge.* Munich: Chr. Kaiser Verlag, 1937.

Dietrich Bonhoeffer Werke. Seventeen Volumes. Gütersloh: Gütersloher, 1987–2012.

Dietrich Bonhoeffer Works. Sixteen Volumes. Fortress, 1996–2012.

---

*A glaring double mistake is repeated three times, when Metaxas has Hitler "democratically elected" as chancellor on January 31 [sic], 1933—on pages 138, 142, and 144. One wonders how he missed the well-known fact that President Hindenburg *appointed* Hitler chancellor on January 30, 1933. See also "Hijacking Bonhoeffer," the excellent review by Clifford Green in *The Christian Century* (October 5, 2010), which laments the many mistakes in Metaxas's volume (rushed into print in time for the sixty-fifth anniversary of Bonhoeffer's death), as well as its bizarre effort to rescue Bonhoeffer for fundamentalist evangelicals and thus rescuing him from the "liberal" thinkers who allegedly "hijacked" him decades ago.

Ethics. Translated by Neville Horton Smith. London: SCM Press, 1955. Originally published as *Ethik*. Munich: Chr. Kaiser Verlag, 1949.

Letters and Papers from Prison. Edited by Eberhard Bethge. New York: Touchstone, 1997. Translation incorporating texts from the third English edition produced by Reginald Fuller, Frank Clark, et al., with additional material by John Bowden. Originally published as *Widerstand und Ergebung: Briefe und Aufzeichnungen auf der Haft*. Munich: Chr. Kaiser Verlag, 1970.

Love Letters from Cell 92: The Correspondence Between Dietrich Bonhoeffer and Maria von Wedemeyer, 1943–45. Edited by Ruth-Alice von Bismarck and Ulrich Itz. Translated by John Brownjohn. Abingdon Press, 1995. Published in German as *Brautbriefe Zelle 92*. Munich: C. H. Beck, 2006, revised edition.

A Testament to Freedom: The Essential Writings of Dietrich Bonhoeffer. Edited by Geffrey B. Kelly and F. Burton Nelson. HarperCollins, 1995, revised edition.

SOME BOOKS ABOUT DIETRICH BONHOEFFER, HANS VON DOHNANYI, AND THEIR FAMILIES

Bethge, Eberhard. *Dietrich Bonhoeffer: A Biography*. Edited by Victoria Barnett. Translated by Eric Mosbacher, Peter and Betty Ross, Frank Clark, and William Glen-Doepel. Minneapolis: Fortress, 2000, 2nd revised edition. Published in German as

Dietrich Bonhoeffer: Eine Biographie. Munich: Chr. Kaiser Verlag, 1967.

Bethge, Eberhard and Renate Bethge, eds. *Last Letters of Resistance: Farewells from the Bonhoeffer Family.* Translated by Dennis Slabaugh. Fortress, 1986.

Leibholz-Bonhoeffer, Sabine. *The Bonhoeffers: Portrait of a Family.* St. Martin's, 1971. Published in German as *Vergangen erlebt überwunden: Schicksale der Familie Bonhoeffer.* Wuppertal: Johanne Kiefel, 1969.

Marty, Martin E. *Dietrich Bonhoeffer's Letters and Papers from Prison: A Biography.* Princeton University Press, 2011.

Metaxas, Eric. *Bonhoeffer: Pastor, Martyr, Prophet, Spy.* Thomas Nelson, 2010.

Meyer, Winfried. *Unternehmen Sieben: Eine Rettungsaktion für vom Holocaust Bedrohte aus dem Amt Ausland/Abwehr in Oberkommando der Wehrmacht.* Frankfurt am Main: Beltz Athenäum, 1993.

Meyer, Winfried, ed. *Verschwörer im KZ: Hans von Dohnanyi und die Häftlinge des 20 Juli 1944 in KZ Sachsenhausen.* Berlin: Edition Hentrich, 1998.

Schlingensiepen, Ferdinand. *Dietrich Bonhoeffer 1906–1945: Martyr, Thinker, Man of Resistance.* Translated by Isabel Best. London: London: T&T Clark, London, 2010. Published in German as *Dietrich Bonhoeffer 1906–1945: Eine Biographie.* Munich: C. H. Beck, 2006.

Smid, Marikje. *Hans von Dohnanyi, Christine Bonhoeffer: Eine Ehe im Widerstand gegen Hitler.* Gütersloh: Gütersloher Verlagshaus, 2002.

Zutt, J., E. Straus, and H. Scheller, eds. *Karl Bonhoeffer: Zum hundertsten Geburtstag 31 März 1968.* Berlin: Springer, 1969.

NOTES

1. Zutt et al., *Karl Bonhoeffer*, p. 49.

2. Bethge and Bethge, *Last Letters of Resistance*, p. 32.

3. Zutt et al., *Karl Bonhoeffer*, p. 91.

4. Ibid., pp. 95ff.

5. *Dietrich Bonhoeffer Werke*, Vol. 9, p. 109.

6. Ibid., pp. 43–44.

7. Smid, *Hans von Dohnanyi, Christine Bonhoeffer*, p. 63. Smid, a theologian, is also a master of historical understanding. Her outstanding work has not been translated, nor is it mentioned in many of the Bonhoeffer books that were written later.

8. Christoph Strohm, *Theologische Ethik im Kampf gegen den Nationalsozialismus: Der Weg Dietrich Bonhoeffers mit den Juristen Hans von Dohnanyi und Gerhard Leibholz in den Widerstand* (Munich: Ch. Kaiser Verlag, 1989), p. 238.

9. Bethge, *Dietrich Bonhoeffer*, p. 34.

10. Zutt et al., *Karl Bonhoeffer*, p. 99.

11. Manfred Wiegandt, "Der Weg Gerhard Leibholz in die Emigration," *Kritische Justiz* 4 (1995), p. 481. See also, by the same author, *Norm und Wirklichkeit: Gerhard Leibholz, 1901–1982: Leben, Werk und Richteramt* (Baden-Baden: Nomos, 1995); and R. Mehring, *Carl Schmitt: Aufstieg und Fall* (Munich: C.H. Beck, 2009), p. 234.

12. Smid, *Hans von Dohnanyi, Christine Bonhoeffer*, p. 81.

13. Bethge, *Dietrich Bonhoeffer*, p. 36.

14. Ibid., pp. 74–75.

15. Ibid., p. 83.

16. Ibid., p. 167.

17. *Dietrich Bonhoeffer Werke*, Vol. 16, p. 366.

18. Bethge, *Dietrich Bonhoeffer*, p. 183.

19. *Dietrich Bonhoeffer Werke*, Vol. 11, pp. 28–29.

20. Bethge, *Dietrich Bonhoeffer*, p. 199.

21. *Dietrich Bonhoeffer Werke*, Vol. 11, pp. 347–348. Bonhoeffer shrewdly used the old German term that was to be made famous by the Nazis; the translator of one Bonhoeffer biographer rendered it as "self-awareness as a people," which doesn't remotely convey the overtones of "*völkische* consciousness." See Schlingensiepen, *Dietrich Bonhoeffer 1906–1945*, p. 90.

22. Uwe Gerrens, *Rüdiger Schleicher: Leben zwischen Staatsdienst und Verschwörung* (Gütersloh: Gütersloher Verlagshaus, 2009), p. 91.

23. *Dietrich Bonhoeffer Werke*, Vol. 12, pp. 50–51.

24. *Dietrich Bonhoeffer Werke*, Vol. 13, p. 34.

25. Zutt et al., *Karl Bonhoeffer*, p. 103.

26. Michael Stolleis, *Geschichte des öffentlichen Rechts in Deutschland, Vol. 3, Staats- und Verwaltungsrechtswissenschaft in Republik und Diktatur 1914–1945* (Munich: C.H. Beck, 1999), pp. 254–299, 333.

27. *Dietrich Bonhoeffer Werke*, Vol. 12, pp. 349–358.

28. Wolfgang Huber and Ilse Tödt, eds., *Ethik im Ernstfall* (Munich: Chr. Kaiser Verlag, 1982), p. 139.

29. Geffrey B. Kelly and F. Burton Nelson, eds., *A Testament to Freedom: The Essential Writings of Dietrich Bonhoeffer* (HarperCollins, 1995), p. 410.

30. Ibid., p. 411.

31. *Dietrich Bonhoeffer Works*, Vol. 13, p. 66.

32. Ekkehard Reitter, *Franz Gürtner, Politische Biographie eines deutschen Juristen: 1881–1941* (Berlin: Duncker & Humblot, 1976).

33. Smid, *Hans von Dohnanyi, Christine Bonhoeffer*, pp. 158, 164.

34. Ibid., pp. 143–145, 251.

35. Ibid., p. 178.

36. Klaus Scholder, *The Churches and the Third Reich, Vol. 2: The Year of Disillusionment: 1934 Barmen and Rome* (London: SCM, 2012), p. 2.

37. *Dietrich Bonhoeffer Werke*, Vol. 13, pp. 169–171.

38. Kelly and Nelson, *A Testament to Freedom*, pp. 230–233.

39. *Dietrich Bonhoeffer Werke*, Vol. 13, p. 179.

40. Ibid., p. 284.

41. Ibid., pp. 272–273.

42. Strohm, *Theologische Ethik im Kampf gegen den Nationalsozialismus*, pp. 254–261.

43. On his later career, see Eckart Conze, Norbert Frei, Peter Hayes, and Moshe Zimmermann, *Das Amt und die Vergangenheit: Deutsche Diplomaten im Dritten Reich und in der Bundesrepublik* (Munich: Blessing, 2010).

44. David Dilks, ed., *The Diaries of Sir Alexander Cadogan, 1938–1945* (London: Cassell, 1971), p. 102.

45. Strohm, *Theologische Ethik im Kampf gegen den Nationalsozialismus*, pp. 240–247.

46. *Dietrich Bonhoeffer Werke*, Vol. 14, p. 247.

47. *Dietrich Bonhoeffer Werke*, Vol. 15, p. 233; Felix Gilbert, *A European Past: Memoirs 1905–1945* (Norton, 1988), pp. 96–97.

48. Smid, *Hans von Dohnanyi, Christine Bonhoeffer*, pp. 245–246.

49. *Dietrich Bonhoeffer Werke*, Vol. 14, p. 303.

50. "After Ten Years," in Kelly and Nelson, *A Testament to Freedom*, p. 485.

51. *Dietrich Bonhoeffer Werke*, Vol. 14, pp. 291–293.

52. Uwe Gerrens, *Medizinisches Ethos und theologische Ethik: Karl und Dietrich Bonhoeffer in der Auseinandersetzung um Zwangssterilisation und "Euthanasie" im Nationalsozialismus* (Munich: Oldenbourg, 1996), pp. 102–118; Smid, *Hans von Dohnanyi, Christine Bonhoeffer*, p. xx; Ian Kershaw, *Hitler, 1936–1945: Nemesis* (Norton, 2000), pp. 426–430.

53. *Dietrich Bonhoeffer Werke*, Vol. 15, pp. 160, 209.

54. *Dietrich Bonhoeffer Werke*, Vol. 16, pp. 48–58.

55. Ibid., p. 75.

56. Christian Hartmann, *Unternehmen Barbarossa: Der deutsche Krieg im Osten 1941–1945* (Munich: Beck, 2011), pp. 62–69 and passim.

57. *Dietrich Bonhoeffer Works*, Vol. 8, p. 49n.

58. Smid, *Hans von Dohnanyi, Christine Bonhoeffer*, p. 20.

59. Meyer, *Unternehmen Sieben*, p. xii.

60. *Dietrich Bonhoeffer Works*, Vol. 8, pp. 37–52.

61. Smid, *Hans von Dohnanyi, Christine Bonhoeffer*, pp. 320–321.

62. *Love Letters from Cell 92*, p. 338; Bonhoeffer and Wedemeyer, *Brautbriefe Zelle 92*, p. 278.

63. Klaus von Dohnanyi, "Rede zur Eröffnung der Ausstellung... in der Paulskirche zu Frankfurt am Main, 25 Januar 1998," in Thomas Vogel, ed., *Der Aufstand des Gewissens* (Hamburg: E. S. Mittler & Sohn, 2000), p. 383.

64. Zutt et al., *Karl Bonhoeffer*, p. 106.

65. *Dietrich Bonhoeffer Works*, Vol. 8, pp. 58–59.

66. Dietrich Bonhoeffer, *Widerstand und Ergebung: Briefe und Aufzeichnungen auf der Haft*, ed. Eberhard Bethge (Munich: Chr. Kaiser Verlag, 1970), p. 34.

67. *Dietrich Bonhoeffer Works*, Vol. 8, p. 69; Smid, *Hans von Dohnanyi, Christine Bonhoeffer*, p. 361.

68. Bethge and Bethge, *Last Letters of Resistance*, pp. 55–57.

69. John W. Wheeler-Bennett, *The Nemesis of Power: The German Army in Politics, 1918–1945* (Viking, 1964), p. 566.

70. *Dietrich Bonhoeffer Works*, Vol. 8, pp. 70–71.

71. Ibid., p. 79.

72. Bethge, *Dietrich Bonhoeffer*, p. 851.

73. Smid, *Hans von Dohnanyi, Christine Bonhoeffer*, pp. 406–407.

74. Ibid., p. 422.

75. *Dietrich Bonhoeffer Works*, Vol. 8, p. 360.

76. Ibid., p. 362.

77. Kelly and Nelson, *A Testament of Freedom*, letter of July 21, 1944, p. 510.

78. *Dietrich Bonhoeffer Works*, Vol. 8, pp. 380, 382–383.

79. Ibid., p. 387.

80. Smid, *Hans von Dohnanyi, Christine Bonhoeffer*, p. 416.

81. Kershaw, *Hitler, 1936–1945: Nemesis*, p. 692.

82. Joachim Fest, *Staatsstreich: Der lange Weg zum 20 Juli* (Munich: btb Verlag), p. 288.

83. Bethge, *Dietrich Bonhoeffer*, appendix.

84. Smid, *Hans von Dohnanyi, Christine Bonhoeffer*, pp. 456–467.

85. Karl-Dietrich Bracher, *Geschichte als Erfahrung* (Munich: DVA, 2001), p. 205.

86. Bethge and Bethge, *Last Letters of Resistance*, pp. 63–64. This is the letter reproduced in the Marbach exhibition and catalog.

87. See Ernst Kaltenbrunner's report to Martin Bormann, "Spiegelbild einer Verschwörung," in *Geheime Dokumente aus dem ehemaligen Reichssicherheitshauptamt*, ed. Hans-Adolf Jacobsen (Stuttgart: Seewald Verlag, 1984), p. 519.

88. Smid, *Hans von Dohnanyi, Christine Bonhoeffer*, p. 445.

89. Ibid., p. 451. See also Gerrens, *Medizinisches Ethos und theologische Ethik*, p. xxx, and Robert L. Reynolds, *A Call for Conscience: Albrecht Tietze's Opposition to Hitler* (Bend, Oregon: Maverick, 2004), chapter 10.

90. Smid, *Hans von Dohnanyi, Christine Bonhoeffer*, p. 453.

91. Bethge and Bethge, *Last Letters of Resistance*, p. 94.

92. Ibid., p. 45.

93. Smid, *Hans von Dohnanyi, Christine Bonhoeffer*, p. 473.

94. *Dietrich Bonhoeffer Works*, Vol. 8, pp. 560–562.

95. Smid, *Hans von Dohnanyi, Christine Bonhoeffer*, p. 474.

96. Tübingen University Archive, 11/09/1947—UAT 443/3. We owe this reference to Simon Taylor.

97. Gerrens, *Medizinisches Ethos und theologische Ethik*, p. 109.

98. See Siegfried Hermle, *Evangelische Kirche und Judentum: Stationen nach 1945* (Göttingen: Vandenhoeck & Ruprecht, 1990), pp. 263ff.

99. Gerhard Leibholz, "Hans von Dohnanyi," in *Der Zwanzigste Juli: Alternative zu Hitler?*, ed., Hans Jürgen Schultz (Berlin: Kreuz, 1974), pp. 139–147. See also Michael Stolleis's splendid *Geschichte des öffentlichen Rechts in Deutschland, Vol. 4, Staats- und Verwaltungsrechtswissenschaft in West und Ost 1945–1990* (Munich: C. H. Beck, 2012). Fabian von Schlabrendorff also returned to Germany and served on the Constitutional Court from 1967 to 1971.

100. See *Aufstand des Gewissens: Militarischer Widerstand gegen Hitler und das NS-Regime 1933–1945*, ed. Thomas Vogel (Hamburg: Mittler & Sohn, 2000), p. 490. The Counter-Intelligence Corps was officially disbanded only in 1961, when it was folded into the US Army's general intelligence units.

101. Jutta Limbach et al., "Erinnerung an Hans von Dohnanyi," *Gedenkstätte Deutscher Widerstand* (2003), p. 14.

102. Bonhoeffer and Wedemeyer, *Brautbriefe Zelle 92*, p. 301.

103. *Dietrich Bonhoeffer Works*, Vol. 8, p. 2.

104. Ibid., p. 6.

105. Ibid., pp. 591–592.

106. Christian Gremmels, in ibid., p. 592.